YARN*play*
at home

NORTH LIGHT BOOKS
CINCINNATI, OHIO

YARN*play*
at home

LISA *shobhana* MASON

YARNPLAY AT HOME. Copyright © 2008 by Lisa Shobhana Mason. Manufac-
tured in China. All rights reserved. It is permissible for the purchaser to make
the projects contained herein and give them away as gifts. No other part of this
book may be reproduced in any form or by any electronic or mechanical means
including information storage and retrieval systems without permission in writing
from the publisher, except by a reviewer, who may quote a brief passage in review.
Published by North Light Books, an imprint of F+W Publications, Inc., 4700 East
Galbraith Road, Cincinnati, Ohio 45236. (800) 289-0963. First edition.
12 11 10 09 08   5 4 3 2 1

Distributed in Canada by Fraser Direct
100 Armstrong Avenue
Georgetown, ON, Canada L7G 5S4
Tel: (905) 877-4411

Distributed in the U.K. and Europe by David & Charles
Brunel House, Newton Abbot, Devon, TQ12 4PU, England
Tel: (+44) 1626 323200, Fax: (+44) 1626 323319
E-mail: postmaster@davidandcharles.co.uk

Distributed in Australia by Capricorn Link
P.O. Box 704, S. Windsor, NSW 2756 Australia
Tel: (02) 4577-3555

Library of Congress Cataloging-in-Publication Data
Mason, Lisa Shobhana.
  YarnPlay at home : handknits for colorful living / by Lisa Shobhana Mason ;
Photography by Brian Steege.
    p. cm.
  Includes index.
  ISBN-13: 978-1-60061-005-9
  1. Knitting. I. Title.
  TT820.M353 2008
  746.43'2--dc22
                          2007028417

EDITOR: **JESSICA GORDON**
ART DIRECTOR AND DESIGNER: **AMANDA DALTON**
PHOTOGRAPHER: **BRIAN STEEGE**
SET STYLIST: **MONICA SKRZELOWSKI**
PRODUCTION COORDINATOR: **GREG NOCK**

fw
F+W PUBLICATIONS, INC.

www.fwbookstore.com

4

This book is dedicated to all my students, past, present and future.

acknowledgments

Thanks to all the amazing bloggers who have supported and inspired me. Your ideas, suggestions and comments have given me invaluable advice and direction about what to do, and most importantly, what not to do, when it comes to knitting.

Thanks to the fabulous women who hosted the *YarnPlay* Blog Tour—Dana Hopings of Knitting Aloud, Lauren "Lolly" Weinhold of Lolly Knitting Around, Wendy Goldstein of Knit and the City, Tracy "Rock Chick" Stewart of Purl Jam, Jacqueline Novoselac of Serendipity and Jamie "Scout" Dixon of Scout's Swag.

Thanks to my editor, Jessica Gordon, and everyone at F+W who supported the *YarnPlay* books.

Jane Wells, you are a lifesaver! Thanks for squeezing the *Knitty Gritty* projects into your busy schedule of school, sports and homework while I cranked out the projects for this book.

I couldn't have finished this book without the help of all the fabulous knitters who generously offered their needles and their time—Sara Wells, Elizabeth Yow, Kirsten Warhoe, Wendy Goldstein and Valerie Lanford.

And, finally, thanks to all the inspiring men and women who are thinking outside the box and looking for new ways to create and craft!

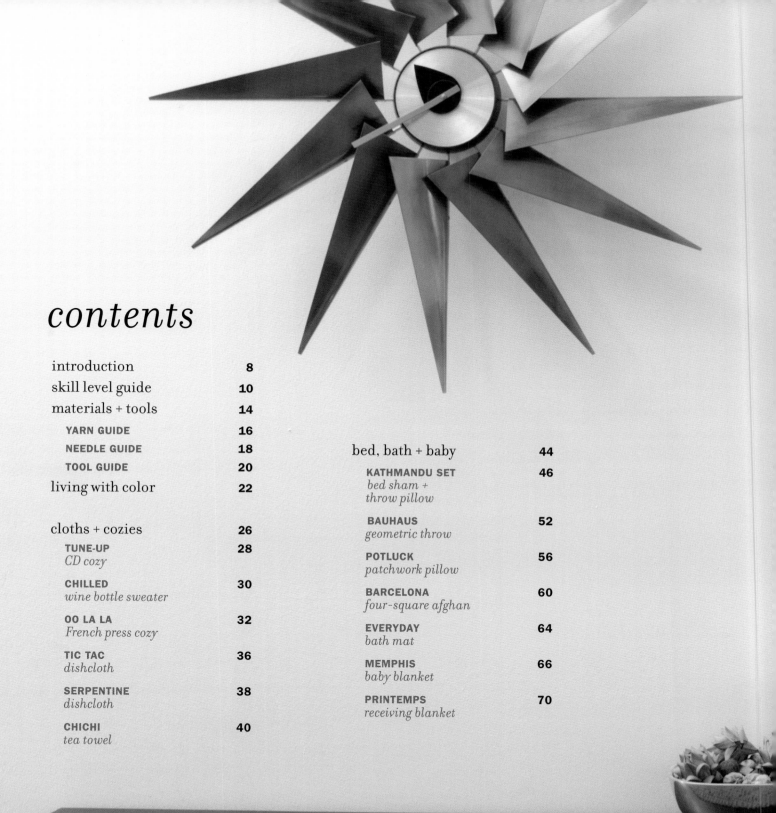

contents

INTRODUCTION

I have a confession to make. When it comes to home decor, I've come late to the party. For most of my life all I really cared about was fashion. I traveled around quite a bit, and I moved just as frequently. And when I was in town, I tended to spend more time hanging out at restaurants and clubs than nesting in my apartment. I wasn't the least bit concerned with decorating my space or even with having a sofa to sit on. In recent years, my life has become a little less nomadic, and I've learned to enjoy spending time at home. It was a bit shocking suddenly to realize that while I had a dozen outfits for every occasion, I owned precious little in the way of things to make me feel comfortable and inspired in my everyday environment. Not being in the position to just go out and buy a truckload of stuff, I had to get creative. First, I made a decision about which things I could compromise on and which I could not. In regard to the latter, I decided it was worthwhile to spend the money on a sofa that I really loved. I was willing to improvise on just about everything else. Today I live in a warm and inviting space that combines a couple of must-have new pieces with loads of vintage finds, all complemented by unique, handknit accessories. Mixing different elements like new and vintage, store-bought and handmade, and a tasteful blend of kitschy and modern gives my space a feeling of vibrancy and warmth.

I've always sought to maintain a personal look that is both unique and stylish, and I now apply that same attitude to my home decor. I aim to keep things flexible and fresh. Home accessories need to be updated in the same way that you keep your wardobe current by adding new items of clothing here and there and blending them with your old favorites. Transforming the look of your home can be as simple as rearranging your furniture and changing the cushion covers and afghans adorning your sofa, chairs or bed.

When it comes to knitting for your home, my advice is to splurge on big showcase pieces like afghans and cushion covers (because with proper care and storage they can last long enough to be passed down to future generations), and use stash yarn for smaller items like cozies and doilies. In addition to adorning your own living space, all the projects in *YarnPlay at Home* make lovely gifts. No matter what your budget, you will find something you can give to even the pickiest recipient. Knit a dishcloth (see pages 36 and 38) and the *Chichi Tea Towel* (see page 40) for your Nana. Knit a one-of-a-kind *Memphis Baby Blanket* (see page 66) for a mother-to-be. Or go all out and knit a *Bauhaus Geometric Throw* (see page 52) as a wedding present for a dear friend. No matter what the item or the occasion, the recipient is sure to love owning an original, handknit work of art! Play around with these patterns, make them your own, and create beautiful pieces that reflect your own unique spirit. I look forward to seeing your creations!

EASY

INTERMEDIATE

ADVANCED

skill level
GUIDE

If you know the basics of knitting, you'll have no problem following any of the patterns in this book. Some of the projects are very, very simple and require only that you know how to knit and sew up seams. Other projects require a few different stitches and techniques. Each project has an icon to let you know the required skill level.

1 STAR　　All you need to know is how to knit, purl and sew seams together.

2 STARS　　Up the ante a little: all of the above plus doing a yarn over and/or working in the round. You'll also need to know techniques like simple crochet and picking up stitches.

3 STARS　　Requires some fancy skills, like intarsia and following a chart.

MATERIALS
+ TOOLS

BEFORE YOU CAST ON, YOU'LL WANT TO MAKE SURE YOU HAVE THE RIGHT MATERIALS AND TOOLS FOR THE PROJECT YOU'VE CHOSEN. In this section, you will find helpful information about yarn and needles, as well as a guide to choosing the right colors for your homey handknits.

yarn
GUIDE

Before you begin knitting a project for the home, consider two important factors: form and function. Form speaks to the aesthetic quality of the project, while function brings up issues of usefulness and durability. Is your primary purpose to create an eye-catching work of art? Or is your purpose to create a piece that can sustain loads of everyday wear and tear? While lofty yarns like cashmere, alpaca and mohair create great drape and are lovely to touch, they are also the least durable. Tightly plied wools and dense cotton can withstand frequent use, but they can be heavy, and in the case of wool, feel rough and scratchy against bare skin. What's a knitter to do? My advice is to first decide whether your primary concern is form or function. Next, take your time choosing the right yarn for your project. Finally, educate yourself on how to care for handknits. With proper care and storage you can extend the life of your handknit accessories (see page 117).

Be sure to check the ball band for care instructions before you make your purchase. If you're not into hand-washing or don't want to spend money on dry cleaning, you probably shouldn't invest in delicate, care-intensive fibers. While superwash wools might be a little more expensive, it's worth it when it means they can go from washer to dryer with no worries!

WOOL AND WOOL BLENDS

These are definitely the most durable yarns and are perfect for afghans and cushion covers that will get a lot of everyday use. Most wool yarns can endure a gentle-cycle, cold-water wash. (Be sure to check the label for care instructions.) However, not all wools can stand up to the heat of a dryer. Only superwash wools are made to withstand both the washer and the dryer, making them a great choice for baby blankets.

COTTON AND COTTON BLENDS

Cotton is perfect for blankets and afghans that will be used during warm weather. It is sturdy enough to be used for bathroom and kitchen rugs. Items that will be washed frequently, like dishcloths and tea towels, should be knit with durable, care-friendly fibers like cotton. Keep in mind that cottons do shrink! Dry them on a low setting and remove them from the dryer while still slightly wet in order to avoid shrinkage. This is the obvious choice for those who are allergic to wool or other animal fibers.

DENIM

Just like your favorite pair of jeans, projects knit with denim yarn will bleed, fade and shrink. Hand-wash items worked in denim yarn in cool water and lay flat to dry. Be sure to prewash the yarn you will use for sewing seams. I, for one, like the well-worn patina of washed denim, but if that look doesn't turn you on, you had better stick to dry cleaning! This fiber is sturdy and fashionable, making it a good choice for handknits for the hipster in your life.

HEMP

Hemp comes from the Cannabis Sativa plant, but don't get any funny ideas—it's not marijuana! It is an incredibly strong plant fiber. High-quality hemp yarn won't shrink, stretch or pill. It can go from the washing machine, on a cold/gentle cycle, to a low temperature in the dryer. This stiff fiber becomes softer with each wash. Its only drawback is that it's a little tough to knit with. However, you can pre-wash hemp yarn before knitting with it to make it easier on your hands.

ALPACA, CASHMERE AND MOHAIR

These luscious fibers are best used on handknits that will be treated with kid gloves (no pun intended). Save them for throws and other accessories that will be used in low-traffic areas of the home. Gently hand-wash items knit in these luxury fibers in cool water and lay flat to dry. The word on the street is that nine out of ten sons, boyfriends and even husbands will not treat these items with the respect they deserve. Save these precious yarns for items that you are knitting for yourself or giving to someone who will really appreciate them!

SILK

Silk is one of the strongest fibers around. It is sturdy, it has a lovely sheen, and in most cases it is slow to pill. Hand-wash it in cool water and lay flat to dry. It is a good choice for items that are destined to be family heirlooms.

GENERAL GUIDELINES FOR YARN WEIGHTS

a **SUPER BULKY** up to 11 sts = 4" (10cm)

b **HEAVY WORSTED** 16 sts = 4" (10cm)

c **CHUNKY/BULKY** 12–15 sts = 4" (10cm)

d **FINGERING/SOCK WEIGHT** 28 sts = 4" (10cm)

e **ARAN/WORSTED WEIGHT** 18–20 sts = 4" (10cm)

f **SPORT WEIGHT** 24 sts = 4" (10cm)

g **DK WEIGHT** 21–22 sts = 4" (10cm)

h **LACE WEIGHT** 32+ sts = 4" (10cm)

Be sure to choose a yarn that gives you the gauge called for in the pattern. Or you can double or even triple strand lighter-weight yarns to attain the required gauge. This is a great way to use up leftover yarn.

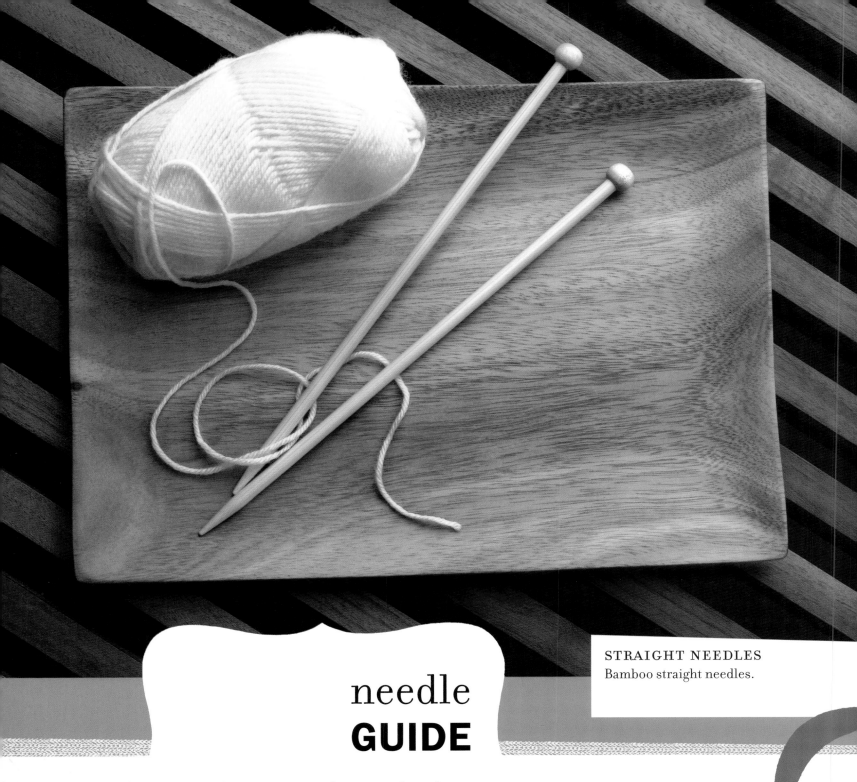

STRAIGHT NEEDLES
Bamboo straight needles.

needle GUIDE

Before you cast on for any project, make sure you have the
right needles. Having the correct needle size for the yarn
you're working with is key to achieving the correct gauge. You
may choose needles made from any material you like. Here's
a guide to choosing the best needle for you.

STRAIGHT VS CIRCULAR

Straight needles are exclusively used for projects that are knit flat. Circular needles are often used to knit in the round, but they can also be used to knit flat pieces. Afghans, other heavy pieces and projects with a large number of cast-on stitches are best suited to circular needles, as they allow you more flexibility and ease of movement, taking the weight of the project off your wrists. Also, projects on circular needles are easier to store, making it a cinch to throw them in your bag so you can knit on the go!

DOUBLE-POINTED NEEDLES

In addition to using double-pointed needles (DPNs) to work in the round, DPNs are perfect for knitting flat projects with a small number of stitches. However, you may want to use point protectors to prevent your stitches from falling off the end!

WHAT'S YOUR TYPE?

Needles can be made from metal, plastic, casein, wood, bamboo or bone.

Those who knit tightly may prefer the smoothness of metal needles, while a loose knitter may get more satisfaction from knitting with bamboo or wood. Also, many synthetic yarns are slippery to knit with and work better paired with bamboo or wood, while natural fibers get the slide they need on metal needles.

METAL NEEDLES are usually made from aluminum. They're super slippery, and the slickest variety can make your knitting quite speedy.

PLASTIC NEEDLES are often the most lightweight and economical choice. They're slightly more slippery than bamboo needles.

CASEIN NEEDLES are made from a milk protein. They're slightly flexible and are less slippery than metal needles.

BAMBOO OR WOODEN NEEDLES "grab" the yarn, keeping stitches steady.

DOUBLE-POINTED NEEDLES
Wooden DPNs courtesy of Laurel Hill.

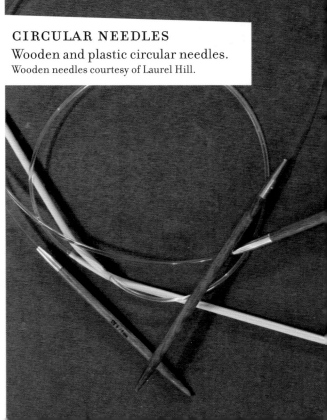

CIRCULAR NEEDLES
Wooden and plastic circular needles.
Wooden needles courtesy of Laurel Hill.

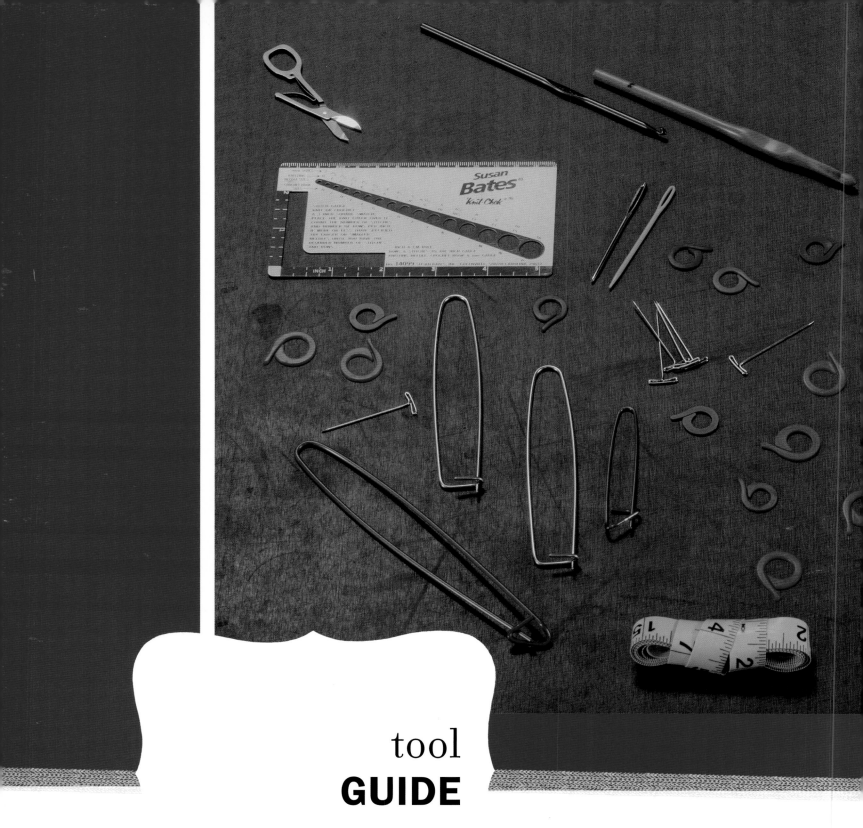

tool
GUIDE

The proper array of tools is essential to fun and pain-free knitting.
Most of the projects in this book are fairly simple, so you can get
away with the bare minimum. But you'll still definitely need a basic
selection. Following is a guide to the general tools you'll need.

**TOOLS CLOCKWISE
FROM TOP LEFT:**
Small scissors, crochet hooks, darning
needles, ring markers, T-pins, tape
measure, stitch holders, stitch gauge.

STITCH GAUGE: This is a little square of plastic with ruled numbers on the sides and an L-shaped cutout along two ruled edges. You can lay the stitch gauge over your knitted swatch and count how many stitches and how many rows fit inside the cutout. Then divide the number of stitches by the number of inches (how long and wide the cutout is) and you've calculated your gauge.

POINT PROTECTORS: These are little eraser-like plastic pieces that slide onto the pointed ends of needles to keep stitches from sliding off.

ROW COUNTER: This small plastic tube has rotating numbers (kind of like those on a combination lock) that let you keep track of your rows.

SCISSORS: You'll always need a pair of scissors. Keep a small pair in your knitting bag.

STITCH HOLDERS: Some are like safety pins without the sharp point. Others open on both ends for easy access. They come in all sizes and allow you to slide stitches off your needles and keep them neatly in place.

TAPE MEASURE: A flexible cloth or plastic tape measure is invaluable to a knitter.

DARNING (YARN) NEEDLE: This is a blunt-tipped needle with a large eye to accommodate yarn. Use a darning needle to sew seams together.

RING MARKERS: These little circles of plastic slide onto your knitting to help you keep track of important spots in your knitting—like the beginning of a round.

RUSTPROOF LOLLIPOP OR T-PINS: These large straight pins are great for securing pieces for blocking.

CROCHET HOOKS: Just like knitting needles, these hooks come in lots of different sizes. Buy a selection and use them to help you pick up dropped stitches and to make crochet borders.

LIVING
with color

Everyone knows color plays a big role in setting a particular mood. It can lift your spirits or it can leave you feeling exhausted and overwhelmed. The same color can even affect people of different temperaments differently. Here are a few questions to ask yourself before choosing a color to work with:

What colors do you respond to in a positive way? What colors totally turn you off?

What mood are you seeking to create in a room? Do you want your handknit piece to blend in or to create contrast?

Now that you have established what vibe you are going for and you know what colors you want to work with and which ones you hope to avoid, use the following guide to fine-tune your choices:

To give a room a more spacious feel, choose airy, neutralizing colors like white, ecru, pale blue and light gray.

To bring warmth to a room, choose sunset shades like red, watermelon, orange and golden yellow.

To cool down a room, use soothing shades of blue, green and gray.

To bring personality to a white room, accentuate it with strong colors like grass green, fire-engine red, royal blue and lemon yellow.

For drama, use bold combinations like black and scarlet or purple and charcoal.

For sophistication, use metallics like silver, gold, copper and bronze.

Don't forget about contrast! A rose-colored room could use a shot of lime or citron. Earth tones will glow when you introduce a metallic accessory.

A QUICK GUIDE TO COLOR

✳✳ **RED** represents the fire element. It stimulates the appetite and brings warmth, energy and passion.

✳✳ **ORANGE** and **YELLOW** are cheerful, enthusiastic and fun. They inspire creativity.

✳✳ **GREEN** represents nature and the earth itself. It is healing and rejuvenating, bringing balance and harmony.

✳✳ **BLUE** represents the ocean and the water element. It is cooling, soothing and tranquil.

✳✳ **PURPLE** has long been associated with royalty. It denotes luxury and spiritual depth.

✳✳ **PINK** raises the spirits. It suggests youthfulness and femininity.

✳✳ **BROWN** represents stability and grounding.

✳✳ **WHITE** indicates cleanliness, clarity and purity.

✳✳ **BLACK**, the color of night, brings intensity, sophistication and glamour.

✳✳ **METALLICS** denote affluence and sophistication.

✳✳ **GRAY** balances and neutralizes stronger colors.

PATTERNS, PATTERNS, PATTERNS!

While color sets the character of a room, patterns give it personality. I find that a lot of people shy away from them because they don't know how to make them work in a room or they are afraid they won't play nicely with other patterns. When combining several patterns, you want them to share a common element, such as color or design. For example, you could use several polka-dot patterns in the same room or you could combine a stripe and a paisley that both contain the same color. I try to avoid having my decor become too matchy-matchy. That's so boring. An unexpected color or pattern makes things pop, adding an air of excitement. What room in your house or apartment could use a little boost?

CLOTHS + COZIES

EVERYONE WHO KNOWS ME OR READS MY BLOG KNOWS I AM CRAZY
FOR COZIES AND CUTE LITTLE HANDKNIT CLOTHS. I love the kitschiness
of dressing up everyday objects like my beloved French press (see the *Oo La La French
Press Cozy*, page 32). And I enjoy the look of wonder and delight on a friend's face when
I present her with a gift covered in a lovely cozy (see the *Tune-Up CD Cozy*, page 28). For
me, it honors the work of my daily chores to perform them with beautiful, handknit
dishcloths (see pages 36 and 38) and tea towels (see page 40). "Serious" knitters often
deem these projects silly. If a project isn't terribly complicated or obviously useful,
they fail to find it worthwhile. But I get tremendous joy from whipping up a sweet little
project. It gives me pleasure to lovingly attend to each detail with the same care and
attention that I would bestow upon a larger project. Cuteness is not a crime! These
cloths and cozies are quick knits meant to bring joy to your knitting and a knowing
smile to your face.

Need a break from your "serious" knitting projects?
Why not try your hand at knitting a cozy? Cozies are great
because they are frivolous, fabulous and totally fun! A little
while ago I found myself in need of a quick and inexpensive
birthday gift for a pal. I burned a mixed CD of some of my
favorite songs, but somehow that just didn't seem like enough.
I wanted to personalize my gift in some way. Thus, the CD cozy
was born. Handmade gifts are great, but handmade wrapping is
the icing on the cake! This cute cozy can be used for gift-giving
or for carrying a favorite CD around in your tote bag.

tune-up
{ CD COZY }

CONSTRUCTION NOTES

This stash-busting project can be knit with leftover bits of sock yarn! When joining a new yarn,
overlap it with the previous yarn and knit with both yarns together for three or four stitches.
Then cut the first yarn, leaving a 1" (3cm) tail, and continue knitting with the new yarn.

MEASUREMENTS
5½" x 5" (14cm x 13cm)

YARN
150 yds (137m) fingering
or sport-weight yarn

a few yards (meters) of yarn
in a contrasting color for edging

NEEDLES + NOTIONS
size US 3 (3.25mm) needles

size D (3.25mm) crochet hook

*If necessary, change needle
size to obtain correct gauge.*

two ½" (1cm) buttons

tapestry needle

sewing needle and thread

GAUGE
26 sts and 51 rows = 4" (10cm) in
garter st on size 3 (3.25mm) needles

CD COZY
Cast on 36 sts. Work in garter st
for 13¾" (35cm).

BUTTONHOLE ROW: K6, yo, k2tog,
work to last 8 sts, k2tog, yo, knit
to end.

Knit 7 rows. Bind off.

FINISHING
With contrast color yarn, work 1 row
of slip st crochet along the edge of
the flap (see page 118 in the Glossary for instructions on working in
slip st crochet).

Fold up the bottom of the Cozy to
approx 5¼" (13cm). Sew the side
seams with a tapestry needle and
scrap yarn. Use a sewing needle and
thread to sew on buttons, aligning
them with the buttonholes.

"*A Wine Bottle Sweater? Whatever for?*" you exclaim. To which I happily reply, "Because it's cute, it's fun, and if you are at all like me you probably have a lot of yarn and a lot of wine bottles lying about." And even if you aren't like me and you don't have too much yarn and too many wine bottles, it is still a cool cozy to accompany a bottle of wine you are taking to a dinner party. Or if you just love kitschy cozies, you can bust out your stash bin, make a few, and use them to decorate a bar or to create a tabletop centerpiece.

chilled
{ WINE BOTTLE SWEATER }

CONSTRUCTION NOTES

The *Wine Bottle Sweater* is knit in the round using double-pointed needles. Worked from the bottom up, simple decreases shape the form-fitting "neck."

MEASUREMENTS

approx 10¼" (26cm) tall

YARN

1 skein Filatura Di Crosa 127 Print (100% wool, 93 yds [85m] per 50g)
   color #14 off-white with tans and browns

Or substitute 60 yds (55m) of any worsted weight yarn.

NEEDLES

size US 8 (5mm) DPNs

If necessary, change needle size to obtain correct gauge.

GAUGE

16 sts and 28 rows = 4" (10cm)

WINE BOTTLE SWEATER

Cast on 36 sts. Divide sts evenly over DPNs. Join for working in the rnd, taking care not to twist sts.

Work in k2, p2 rib for 8 rnds.

Change to St st, inc 2 sts evenly spaced over next rnd—38 sts.

Work even until piece measures 8" (20cm), or desired body length from cast-on edge.

DECREASE FOR TOP

RND 1: * K4, k2tog; rep from * to last 2 sts, k2—32 sts.

RNDS 2–3: Knit.

RND 4: * K2, k2tog; rep from * to end of rnd—24 sts.

RNDS 5–6: Knit.

RND 7: * K2, k2tog; rep from * to end of rnd—18 sts.

RNDS 8–9: Knit.

RND 10: K7, k2tog twice—16 sts.

Work in k2, p2 rib for 8 rnds. Bind off.

31

When I was drawing up the project list for YarnPlay at Home, I asked my blog readers what kind of cozy pattern they would most like to see in a book, and the majority of those who responded suggested a French press cozy. And voilá, the *Oo La La French Press Cozy* was born! I love the idea of adorning objects that I use on a daily basis. Whether your mission is to cleverly conceal your French press or to bring a shot of color to your kitchen countertop, this cozy is super-cute and quick to knit.

oo la la
{ FRENCH PRESS COZY }

CONSTRUCTION NOTES
The body of the *French Press Cozy* is knit as a flat piece of fabric. After seaming and transferring the stitches to double-pointed needles, you will work the top portion in the round.

MEASUREMENTS
10½" (27cm) high x
12" (30cm) around

YARN
1 skein of Scout's Swag Superwash Worsted (100% merino wool, 175 yds [160m])
> color Blue in Green

Or substitute 150 yds (137m) of any worsted weight yarn.

NEEDLES + NOTIONS
size US 8 (5mm) straight needles

size US 8 (5mm) DPNs

If necessary, change needle size to obtain correct gauge.

tapestry needle

GAUGE
18 sts and 28 rows = 4" (10cm) in patt

FRENCH PRESS COZY

With straight needles, CO 54 sts.

BEGIN PATTERN

ROW 1: K1, kfb in each st to last st, k1.

ROW 2: K1, * k2tog, p2tog; rep from * to last st, k1.

Rep Rows 1–2 until piece measures 6¾" (17cm), ending with Row 2.

Knit 8 rows.

Leaving yarn attached, place sts on a piece of waste yarn.

Leaving an open space for the handle, sew the side seam above and below the handle.

Place sts on DPNs. Remove waste yarn.

Knit 2 rnds.

TOP DECREASES

RND 1: * K7, k2tog; rep from * to end of rnd—48 sts.

RNDS 2–3: Knit.

RND 4: * K6, k2tog; rep from* to end of rnd—42 sts.

RND 5: Knit.

RND 6: * K5, k2tog; rep from * to end of rnd—36 sts.

RND 7: Knit.

RND 8: * K4, k2tog; rep from * to end of rnd—30 sts.

RND 9: Knit.

RND 10: * K3, k2tog; rep from * to end of rnd—24 sts.

RND 11: Knit.

RND 12: * K2, k2tog; rep from * to end of rnd—18 sts.

RND 13: Knit.

RND 14: * K1, k2tog; rep from * to end of rnd—12 sts.

Knit 5 rnds.

FINAL RND: K2tog around—6 sts.

Cut yarn and pull through rem sts. Finish off. Weave in ends.

tic tac
{ DISHCLOTH }

A dishcloth is the perfect project to knit on the go!
Knit a few rows on your subway ride to work or while you're waiting for an appointment. Inexpensive and quick to knit, a dishcloth is the perfect little project on which to perfect your knitting skills. You may want to keep a few extra on hand, because these sweet dishcloths make great gifts.

CONSTRUCTION NOTES

The Tic Tac pattern is perfect for beginners. It's a simple four-row repeating pattern that differs only slightly from row to row. Try the *Serpentine Dishcloth* (see page 38) when you are ready for more of a challenge.

MEASUREMENTS
11" x 11" (28cm x 28cm)

YARN
1 skein Lion Brand Lion Cotton (100% cotton, 189 yds [170m] per 113g)
    color #257 Cornmeal

Or substitute 140 yds (128m) of any worsted weight cotton.

NEEDLES
size US 6 (4mm) needles

If necessary, change needle size to obtain correct gauge.

GAUGE
16 sts and 24 rows = 4" (10cm) in patt

DISHCLOTH
CO 42 sts.

Knit 2 rows.

BEGIN PATTERN

ROW 1: K3, p1, * k1, p1; rep from * to last 2 sts, k2.

ROW 2: K2, * p1, k1; rep from * to last 2 sts, k2.

ROW 3: K2, * p1, k1; rep from * to last 2 sts, k2.

ROW 4: K3, p1, * k1, p1; rep from * to last 2 sts, k2.

Rep Rows 1–4 until piece measures approx 10½" (27cm), ending with Row 4.

Knit 2 rows. Bind off. Weave in ends.

serpentine
{ **DISHCLOTH** }

This lovely dishcloth is perfect for a new knitter who is up for a challenge, but who isn't ready to invest a lot of time or a load of cash into her next project. And more experienced knitters can whip this up in no time!

CONSTRUCTION NOTES

The yarn overs and decreases in this pattern create pretty peek-a-boo eyelets, and the staggered knits and purls produce dimensional ribs.

MEASUREMENTS
11" x 11" (28cm x 28cm)

YARN
1 skein of Lion Brand Lion Cotton
(100% cotton, 236 yds [212m]
per 113g)
    color #157 Sunflower

*Or substitute 140 yds (128m)
of any worsted weight cotton yarn.*

NEEDLES
size US 6 (4mm) needles

*If necessary, change needle size
to obtain correct gauge.*

GAUGE
16 sts and 24 rows = 4" (10cm)
in St st

DISHCLOTH
CO 42 sts.

Knit 2 rows.

BEGIN PATTERN

ROW 1 (RS): K2, p2, * yo, k1, yo, p2;
rep from * to last 2 sts, k2.

ROW 2 (WS): K4, * p3, k2; rep from *
to last 2 sts, k2.

ROW 3: K2, p2, * k3, p2; rep from *
to last 2 sts, k2.

ROW 4: K4, * p3tog, k2; rep from *
to last 2 sts, k2.

Rep Rows 1–4 until piece measures
approx 10½" (27cm), ending with
Row 4.

Knit 2 rows. Bind off.
Weave in ends.

chichi
{ TEA TOWEL }

In the case of this bright dish towel, "Chichi" is short for cheap and cheerful. If you are pressed for money or time, this is the perfect project! It's portable enough to take with you when you travel, and it's simple enough to serve as TV knitting. Paired with a handknit dishcloth, it makes a great gift. You could also pair this towel with a washcloth-sized version and use it in a guest bathroom.

CONSTRUCTION NOTES

The *Chichi Tea Towel* is easy to knit, but the optional crochet border raises the skill level to 2 stars.

MEASUREMENTS
16" x 21" (41cm x 53cm)

YARN
1 skein Lion Brand Lion Cotton (100% cotton, 236 yds [212m] per 113g)
> color #108 Morning Glory Blue

several yards (meters) of yarn in a contrasting color for edging

Or substitute 236 yds (212m) of any worsted weight cotton yarn.

NEEDLES + HOOKS
size US 7 (4.5mm) needles

If necessary, change needle size to obtain correct gauge.

size G (4.25mm) crochet hook

GAUGE
16 sts and 24 rows = 4" (10cm) in patt on size US 7 (4.5mm) needles

TEA TOWEL
Cast on 63 sts. Knit 2 rows.

BEGIN PATTERN

ROW 1: K10, p3, (k7, p3) 4 times, k10.

ROW 2: K3, (p7, k3) 6 times.

Rep Rows 1–2 until piece measures 20½" (52cm) from cast-on edge, ending with Row 2.

Knit 2 rows. Bind off.

FINISHING
With contrast color yarn, work 1 rnd of single crochet around edges. (See page 118 in the Glossary for instructions on working a single crochet border.)

BED, BATH + BABY

ON ANY GIVEN SATURDAY, YOU MIGHT FIND ME STROLLING AROUND A MUSEUM OR GALLERY. I enjoy viewing artists' unique interpretations of universal themes and elements, and I am always drawn to the repetition of various designs throughout the ages. They make an impression upon my consciousness, and consequently, they sometimes emerge in my own work. From the bold, outsider art vibe of the Gee's Bend quilts and the austerity of the Bauhaus movement to the vivacious designs of the late 1960s, great works and movements serve as influence and inspiration for the designs in this chapter. For example, the *Memphis Baby Blanket* (see page 66) pays homage to one of my favorite Gee's Bend artists. And the *Barcelona Four-Square Afghan* (see page 60) is my tribute to a popular design motif from the 1960s and 1970s. You can follow the patterns as they are written or play around and create a design or color arrangement that speaks to your spirit.

There is nothing that I treasure more than a good night's sleep. Creating a haven of comfort and beauty in my bedroom is essential to my well-being. When I designed the Kathmandu sham and matching pillow, I envisioned a pampered princess reclining on a lofty bed covered with sumptuous linens and big, fluffy pillows. This enchanting set will bring a feeling of luxury to even the most boring bedroom. Sweet dreams!

kathmandu set
{ BED SHAM + THROW PILLOW }

CONSTRUCTION NOTES

One skein of Lorna's Laces Heaven makes both the sham and the smaller pillow. Unexpected bumps of knit-and-purl in the middle of smooth Stockinette stitch create surprising texture in these luxurious pillow covers.

BED SHAM

MEASUREMENTS
25" x 19" (64cm x 48cm)

YARN
1 skein Lorna's Laces Heaven (mohair/nylon blend, 975 yds [891m] per 198g)
  color Black Purl

1 skein makes the Bed Sham *and the* Throw Pillow.

NEEDLES + NOTIONS
29" to 32" (74cm to 81cm) size US 8 (5mm) circular needles

If necessary, change needle size to obtain correct gauge.

four 1" (3cm) buttons

tapestry needle

safety pins

sewing needle and thread

GAUGE
16 sts and 26 rows = 4" (10cm) in St st

Gauge is the same for the Bed Sham *and the* Throw Pillow.

THROW PILLOW

MEASUREMENTS
14" x 17" (36cm x 43cm)

NEEDLES + NOTIONS
size US 8 (5mm) circular needles

If necessary, change needle size to obtain correct gauge.

three 1" (3cm) buttons

tapestry needle

safety pins

sewing needle and thread

See Bed Sham *for yarn and gauge information.*

BED SHAM

FRONT
Cast on 75 sts.

Knit 4 rows.

BEGIN PATTERN

ROW A (RS): Knit.

ROW B (WS): K3, purl to last 3 sts, k3.

Rep Rows A–B until piece measures 3"
(8cm), ending with Row B.

ROW C (RS): K14, p1, * k1, p1; rep from *
to last 14 sts, k14.

ROW D (WS): K3, p12, * k1, p1; rep from
* to last 14 sts, p11, k3.

Rep Rows C–D 6 times.

ROW E (RS): K14, p1, (k1, p1) 4 times,
k29, p1, (k1, p1) 4 times, k14.

ROW F (WS): K3, p12, (k1, p1) 4 times,
p30, (k1, p1) 4 times, p11, k3.

Rep Rows E–F until piece measures 20"
(51cm) from cast-on edge, ending with
Row F.

Rep Rows C–D 7 times.

Rep Rows A–B until piece measures
24½" (62cm) from cast-on edge, ending
with Row B.

Knit 4 rows. Place a safety pin at each
end of last row to mark start of Flap.

FLAP
Rep Rows A–B until piece measures 32"
(81cm) from cast-on edge, ending with
Row B.

BUTTONHOLE ROW (RS): K7, (k2tog, yo
twice, k2tog, k15) 3 times, k2tog, yo
twice, k2tog, k7.

NEXT ROW: K3, purl to last 3 sts, k3.

NEXT ROW: K3, * p1, k1; rep from * to
last 4 sts, p1, k3.

Rep last row 5 times.

Bind off.

BACK
Cast on 75 sts. Knit 4 rows.

BEGIN PATTERN

ROW A (RS): Knit.

ROW B (WS): K3, purl to last 3 sts, k3.

Rep Rows A–B until piece measures
24½" (62cm), ending with Row 2.

Knit 4 rows. Bind off.

FINISHING
Seam the bottom and sides of the Front
and Back pieces using a tapestry needle
and scrap yarn. Use a sewing needle and
thread to sew on buttons, aligning them
with the buttonholes. Weave in ends.

THROW PILLOW

The *Throw Pillow* is knit in one piece beginning at the top of the Back.

Cast on 55 sts.

Knit 4 rows.

BEGIN PATTERN

ROW A (RS): Knit.

ROW B (WS): K3, purl to last 3 sts, k3.

Rep Rows A–B until piece measures 13½" (34cm), ending with Row B.

Knit 4 rows, then place a safety pin at beg and end of row to mark bottom edge of Pillow.

Knit 4 rows.

Rep Rows A–B until piece measures 18" (46cm), ending with Row B.

ROW C (RS): K15, * p1, k1; rep from * to last 16 sts, p1, k15.

ROW D (WS): K3, p13, * k1, p1; rep from * to last 15 sts, p12, k3.

Rep Rows C–D until piece measures 24" (61cm), ending with Row D.

Rep Rows A–B until piece measures 27½" (70cm), ending with Row B.

Knit 4 rows, then place a safety pin at beg and end of row to mark top of Pillow.

FLAP

Rep Rows A–B until piece measures 32" (81cm), ending with Row B.

BUTTONHOLE ROW (RS): K12, k2tog, yo twice, k2tog, k23, k2tog, yo twice, k2tog, k12.

NEXT ROW: K3, purl to last 3 sts, k3.

NEXT ROW: K3, * p1, k1; rep from * to last 4 sts, p1, k3.

Rep last row 5 times.

Bind off.

FINISHING

Use a tapestry needle and scrap yarn to sew the side seams as marked by the safety pins. Use a sewing needle and thread to sew on buttons to align with the buttonholes. Weave in ends.

bauhaus
{ GEOMETRIC THROW }

When I designed this blanket, I was thinking of the Bauhaus art movement with its stern and unadorned style. My aim was to create a piece that is both sleek and clean, as well as moody and sumptuous. This inviting throw adds warmth to an ultra-modern decor without causing distraction, giving the *Bauhaus Geometric Throw* a twenty-first-century look.

CONSTRUCTION NOTES
The squares are arranged so that one color shows horizontal garter ridges and the other vertical ridges.

MEASUREMENTS
52" x 52" (132cm x 132cm)

Throw is comprised of 4 26" x 26" (66cm x 66cm) squares.

YARN
1 skein Lorna's Laces Heaven (mohair/nylon blend, 975 yds [891m] per 198g) in each of the foll colors:

> *color Pewter (A)*
> *color Blackberry (B)*

Or substitute 975 yds (891m) of any worsted weight mohair yarn for each color.

NEEDLES + NOTIONS
29" to 32" (74cm to 80cm) size US 10 (6mm) circular needle

If necessary, change needle size to obtain correct gauge.

tapestry needle

GAUGE
14 sts and 28 rows = 4" (10cm) in garter st

GEOMETRIC THROW

Cast on 92 sts. Work in garter st until square measures 26" (66cm).

Bind off.

Knit 2 squares with Color A and 2 squares with Color B.

FINISHING
Sew squares together with mattress stitch, turning one pair of colors so that the garter ridges run vertically. (See page 120 in the Glossary for illustrated instructions on working in mattress stitch.)

The Potluck Patchwork Pillow *is a stash-busting project that combines different colors and textures to create a unique take on a traditional design.* I chose one of my favorite colors, in merino wool, to use as the main color. Next, for a different texture I added a silk/mohair blend as one of two contrast colors. I purposely chose a color that was only partly complementary to the main color. I find that working with colors that are slightly off brings a bit of depth to the project at hand. For the second contrast color I double-stranded leftover bits of sport-weight yarn. I chose the colors randomly from my stash, creating a "potluck" effect. This is a great way to use up leftover bits of sock yarn!

potluck
{ PATCHWORK PILLOW }

CONSTRUCTION NOTES

Each of the five vertical strips is made of five squares and is knit in one piece, starting from the bottom. The button bands are double-sided, separated by a turning ridge. On the front you will pick up stitches along the top border of the five strips to create the button band. The back is knit in one piece starting with the bottom and ending with the button band at the top.

MEASUREMENTS
14" x 14" (36cm x 36cm)

YARN
1 skein Lorna's Laces Shepherd Worsted (100% superwash wool, 225 yds [206m] per 113g)
   color Pink Blossom (MC)

Or substitute 225 yds (206m) of any worsted weight yarn.

1 skein Rowan Kidsilk Haze (mohair/silk blend, 227 yds [207m] per 25g), working with 2 strands held tog
   color 632 Hurricane (CC1)

Or substitute 100 yds (91m) of a single strand of any lightweight yarn.

approx 250 yds (228m) of fingering/ sport weight scrap yarn, working with 2 strands held tog
   variegated scrap yarns (CC2)

Or substitute 120 yds (110m) of a single strand of any worsted weight yarn.

NEEDLES + NOTIONS
size US 8 (5mm) needles

If necessary, change needle size to obtain correct gauge.

five ⅞" (2cm) buttons

one 14" x 14" (36cm x 36cm) pillow insert

tapestry needle

sewing needle and thread

GAUGE
19 sts and 28 rows = 4" (10cm) in St st with MC

PATCHWORK PILLOW

FRONT

The Front of the Pillow is knit in 5 separate vertical strips, knit from the bottom up. For each strip, cast on 14 sts and work in St st in the color indicated by the chart until the square measures 2¾" (7cm) long, ending with a WS row.

Change colors and rep until you have completed 5 squares. Bind off. Keep 1 st at beg and end of every row in garter st, and work first 2 and last 2 rows of each strip in garter st.

Using mattress stitch, seam strips together as indicated by the chart. (See page 120 in the Glossary for instructions on working in mattress stitch.)

BUTTON BAND

With MC, pick up and knit 66 sts across top edge of Front. (See page 120 in the Glossary for instructions on picking up sts.)

Work 3 rows in St st, beg with a purl row.

BUTTONHOLE ROW (RS): K5, (yo, k2tog, k12) twice, (k2tog, yo, k12) twice, k2tog, yo, k5.

Beg with a purl row, cont in St st for 4 rows.

TURNING RIDGE

Knit next row (WS) for Turning Ridge. Cont in St st, beg with a knit row, for 4 rows.

NEXT ROW: Rep Buttonhole Row.

Beg with a purl row, cont in St st for 3 rows. Bind off.

BACK

With MC, cast on 66 sts.

Knit 2 rows.

ROW 1: Knit.

ROW 2: K3, purl to last 3 sts, k3.

Rep Rows 1–2 until piece measures 13¾" (35cm).

Knit 2 rows.

BUTTON BAND

Change to CC2. Beg with a knit row, work 9 rows of St st.

TURNING RIDGE

Knit next row (WS) for Turning Ridge. Cont in St st, beg with a knit row, for 8 rows.

Bind off.

FINISHING

Seam the Back and Front of the Pillow tog.

Fold each Button Band to WS on Turning Ridge. With yarn threaded on a tapestry needle, slip stitch the Button Band in place.

Attach the buttons opposite buttonholes with a sewing needle and thread. Weave in any ends.

Potluck Patchwork Pillow *Diagram*

MC	CC2	MC	CC2	MC
CC2	CC1	CC2	CC1	CC2
CC1	CC2	MC	CC2	CC1
CC2	CC1	CC2	CC1	CC2
MC	CC2	MC	CC2	MC

This pattern of interlocking squares is often seen in designs from the late 1960s and early 1970s. I have seen it on carpets, curtains and fabric. Sometimes it looks terribly tacky, and at other times it looks super sophisticated. I love designs that give you pause and really make you think about whether or not they appeal to you. There are so many ways you can play around with this pattern. You could use the same main color for all of the squares or use several colors instead of just one contrast color. Feel free to interpret this design and make it your own!

barcelona
{ FOUR-SQUARE AFGHAN }

CONSTRUCTION NOTES

This afghan is composed of sixteen individually knit squares. Knit them as indicated by the charts and arrange accordingly. Intarsia charts are read from right to left on odd-numbered rows, and from left to right on even-numbered rows. Usually all the stitches on odd-numbered rows are knit, and those on even-numbered rows are purled. However, for this design you will knit the first two and last two stitches on every row. Make sure to pay close attention to the pattern, as it calls for knitting some rows to create a garter stitch border.

MEASUREMENTS
48" x 57" (122cm x 145cm)

YARN
3 skeins Rowan Scottish Tweed Chunky (100% wool, 109 yds [100m] per 100g) in each of the following colors:

    color #024 Porridge
    color #023 Midnight
    color #017 Lobster
    color #007 Lewis Gray
    color #026 Rose

Or substitute 327 yds (299m) of any chunky-weight wool for each color listed above.

NEEDLES + NOTIONS
size US 11 (8mm) needles

If necessary, change needle size to obtain correct gauge.

tapestry needle

GAUGE
12 sts and 18 rows = 4" (10cm) in St st

FOUR-SQUARE AFGHAN

Each large square is composed of 4 smaller squares. For each smaller square, cast on 36 sts with the color indicated and foll the chart for that particular square. Knit the first and last 2 sts of each row, plus knit every st of the foll rows: 1, 2, 63 and 64, to make a garter st border.

FINISHING

Block each square before seaming. Seam squares tog with mattress stitch according to the Construction Diagram. (See the Glossary, page 120, for instructions on working in mattress stitch.) Weave in any ends.

KEY

Square A:	MC = Porridge
	CC1 = Midnight
	CC2 = Lobster
Square B:	MC = Rose
	CC1 = Midnight
	CC2 = Porridge
Square C:	MC = Lewis Gray
	CC1 = Midnight
	CC2 = Rose
Square D:	MC = Lobster
	CC1 = Midnight
	CC2 = Lewis Gray

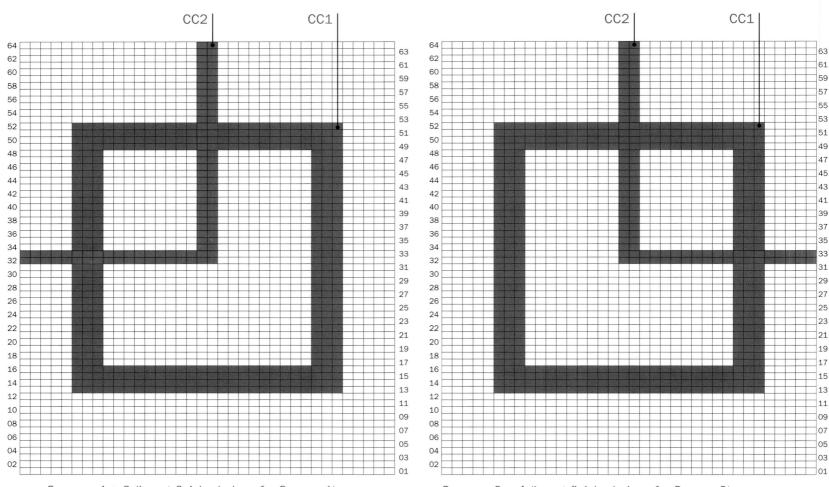

Squares 1 + 3 (Invert finished piece for Square 1)

Squares 2 + 4 (Invert finished piece for Square 2)

KEY

☐ = MC

▨ = CC1

▨ = CC2

Knit on odd-numbered rows; purl on even-numbered rows.

Note the foll exceptions: Knit the first and last 2 sts on every row.

Rows 1, 2, 63, 64 knit every st.

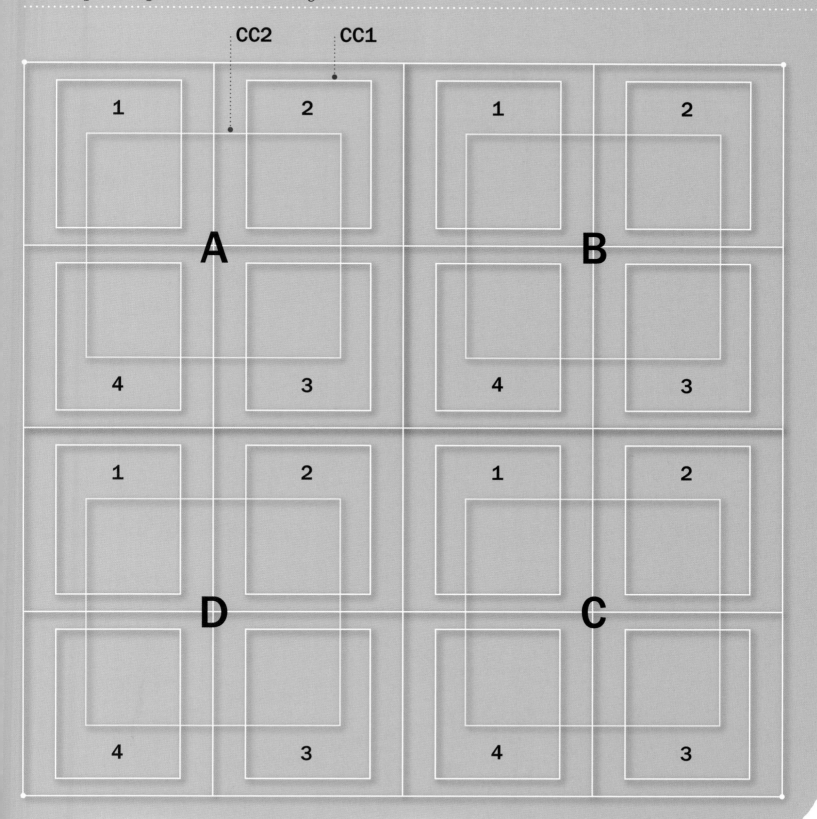

everyday
{ BATH MAT }

I have yet to meet a knitter who doesn't have a family member or close friend whom they really want to knit for, but who complains that all sweaters are scratchy and that just the thought of wearing handknit socks makes her feet sweat! Everyone can use an *Everyday Bath Mat.* Both novices and seasoned knitters alike will find this easy and elegant project fun to knit.

CONSTRUCTION NOTES
You will be knitting with two strands of yarn held together throughout this simple striped seed stitch pattern.

MEASUREMENTS
22" x 32" (56cm x 81cm)

YARN
2 skeins Lion Brand Lion Cotton
(100% cotton, 236 yds [212m] per 113g)
  color # 98 Natural

Or substitute 472 yds (431m) of any worsted weight cotton yarn.

NEEDLES
29" to 32" (74cm to 81cm) size
US 10½ (6.5mm) circular needle

If necessary, change needle size to obtain correct gauge.

GAUGE
Working with 2 strands held tog,
14 sts and 22 rows = 4" (10cm)
in patt

BATH MAT
Using 2 strands of yarn held tog, cast on 73 sts. Knit 2 rows.

BEGIN PATTERN

ROW 1 (RS): K6, * (k1, p1) 3 times, k5; rep from * to last st, k1.

ROW 2 (WS): K1, * p5, (p1, k1) 3 times; rep from * to last 6 sts, p5, k1.

Rep Rows 1–2 until piece measures approx 31½" (80cm), ending with Row 1.

Knit 2 rows. Bind off. Weave in any ends.

65

memphis
{ BABY BLANKET }

My inspiration for this blanket was a quilt created by the Gee's Bend artist, Polly Bennett. My initial impulse was to create a literal, knitted interpretation of her quilt, but then, almost immediately, I became bored with that idea. I set my sketches aside for a few days, and when I picked them up again I felt inspired to create a design that paid homage to Ms. Bennett's work while reflecting my own spirit and aesthetic. Similarly, I hope that you will take inspiration from my design and use it as a springboard to find a pattern that speaks to you.

CONSTRUCTION NOTES

Knit squares in the sequence indicated if you want to keep color continuity from one square to the next. Or not! My design is merely a suggestion. Play around with the arrangement of the squares and see what emerges.

MEASUREMENTS
30" x 30" (76cm x 76cm)

YARN
2 skeins Debbie Bliss Merino Aran (100% merino wool, 85 yds [77m] per 50g) in each of the foll colors:
    color #208 lavender (A)
    color #702 grape (B)

Or substitute 172 yds (157m) of any worsted weight yarn for each color.

2 skeins of Noro Kureyon (100% wool, 110 yds [100m] per 50g) in each of the foll colors:
    color #52 blue/violet/chartreuse (C)
    color #147 blues/greens (D)
    color #166 green/teal/pink/purple (E)

Or substitute 220 yds (201m) of any worsted weight yarn for each color.

NEEDLES + NOTIONS
size US 8 (5mm) needles

If necessary, change needle size to obtain correct gauge.

tapestry needle

GAUGE
18 sts and 30 rows = 4" (10cm) in garter st

BABY BLANKET

SQUARE 1
With E, cast on 40 sts. Work in garter st for 3" (8cm). Change to A, work in garter st for 3" (8cm). Change to C, work in garter st for 3" (8cm). Bind off.

SQUARE 2
With A, cast on 40 sts. Work in garter st for 3" (8cm). Change to C, work in garter st for 3" (8cm). Change to B, work in garter st for 3" (8cm). Bind off.

SQUARE 3
With E, cast on 40 sts. Work in garter st for 3" (8cm). Change to B, work in garter st for 3" (8cm). Change to D, work in garter st for 3" (8cm). Bind off.

SQUARE 4
With D, cast on 40 sts. Work in garter st for 3" (8cm). Change to A, work in garter st for 3" (8cm). Change to C, work in garter st for 3" (8cm). Bind off.

SQUARE 5
With C, cast on 40 sts. Work in garter st for 3" (8cm). Change to B, work in garter st for 3" (8cm). Change to E, work in garter st for 3" (8cm). Bind off.

SQUARE 6
With B, cast on 40 sts. Work in garter st for 3" (8cm). Change to C, work in garter st for 3" (8cm). Change to A, work in garter st for 3" (8cm). Bind off.

SQUARE 7
With D, cast on 40 sts. Work in garter st for 3" (8cm). Change to A, work in garter st for 3" (8cm). Change to E, work in garter st for 3" (8cm). Bind off.

SQUARE 8
With D, cast on 40 sts. Work in garter st for 3" (8cm). Change to B, work in garter st for 3" (8cm). Change to C, work in garter st for 3" (8cm). Bind off.

SQUARE 9
With A, cast on 40 sts. Work in garter st for 3" (8cm). Change to E, work in garter st for 3" (8cm). Change to B, work in garter st for 3" (8cm). Bind off.

FINISHING
Block squares to 9¼" x 9¼" (23cm x 23cm). Seam squares tog as indicated.

BORDER
With RS facing and using D, pick up and knit 123 sts along side I. (See the Glossary, page 120, for instructions on picking up sts.) Work in seed st for 9 rows, inc 1 st at each end of every other row, working inc into the patt. (See the Glossary, page 121, for instructions on working in seed st.) Bind off.

With RS facing and using C, pick up and knit 123 sts along side II. Work in seed st for 9 rows, inc 1 st at each end of every other row, working inc into the patt. Bind off.

With RS facing and using D, pick up and knit 123 sts along side III. Work in seed st for 9 rows, inc 1 st at each end of every other row, working inc into the patt. Bind off.

With RS facing and using E, pick up and knit 123 sts along side IV. Work in seed st for 9 rows, inc 1 st at each end of every other row, working inc into the patt. Bind off.

Seam corners of border. Weave in ends.

KEY

A	Debbie Bliss *merino aran 208 lavender*
B	Debbie Bliss *merino aran 702 grape*
C	Kureyon 52
D	Kureyon 147
E	Kureyon 166

Memphis Baby Blanket *Construction Diagram*

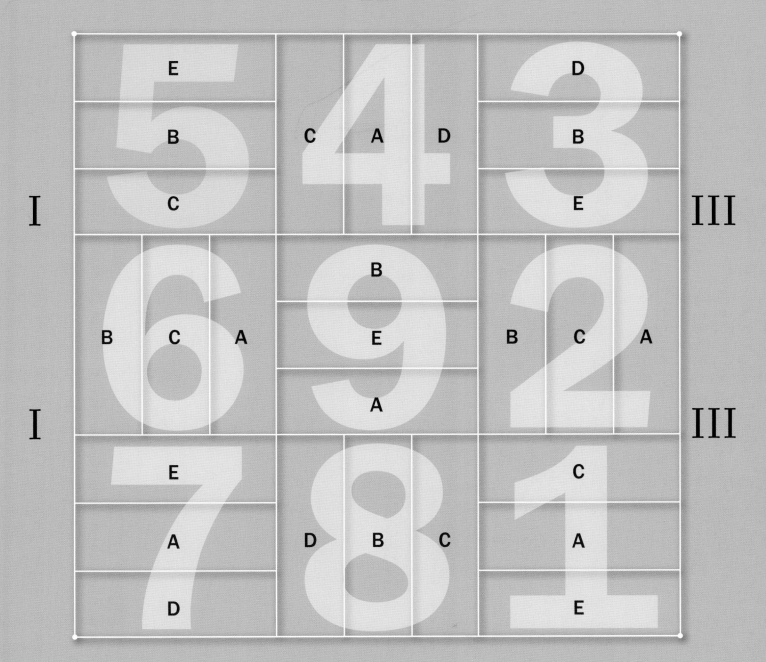

printemps
{ RECEIVING BLANKET }

It is no secret that I love color! However, every now and then I like a little texture, too. When combining both elements, it is usually best to keep things simple. Less is definitely more when working with a variegated color. A simple textured stitch allows the beauty of a hand-dyed yarn to speak for itself. The combination is pleasing to both the hand and the eye. A simple crocheted border gives definition and a polished finish to this sweet receiving blanket.

CONSTRUCTION NOTES

Experiment with the crocheted border. You may use more rounds, or fewer, until you find the look you like best.

MEASUREMENTS
approx 29" x 29" (74cm x 74cm)

YARN
7 skeins of Artyarns Supermerino
(100% merino, 104 yds [95m] per 50g)
> color #sm105 variegated
> pink and green (MC)

*Or substitute 728 yds (665m)
of any aran/worsted weight
wool yarn.*

1 skein of Artyarns Supermerino
> color #sm214 rose (CC)

*Or substitute 104 yds (95m) of
any aran/worsted weight wool yarn.*

NEEDLES + HOOKS
size US 9 (5.5mm) needles

*If necessary, change needle
size to obtain correct gauge.*

size I (5.5mm) crochet hook

GAUGE
18 sts and 28 rows = 4" (10cm) in
patt on size US 9 (5.5mm) needles

RECEIVING BLANKET

With MC, cast on 126 sts.

Knit 2 rows.

BEGIN PATTERN

ROW 1 (RS): Knit.

ROW 2 (WS): K2, * k1, p1; rep from * to last 2 sts, k2.

ROW 3: Knit.

ROW 4: K2, * p1, k1; rep from * to last 2 sts, k2.

Rep Rows 1–4 until piece measures approx 27½" (70cm), ending with Row 4.

Knit 2 rows. Bind off.

FINISHING

Block Blanket before adding crochet border.

With CC, work 1 rnd of slip st crochet, followed by 2 rnds of single crochet around the edges. (See the Glossary, page 118, for instructions on working in slip st and single crochet.)

HOUSE
+ HOME

WHEN SOMEONE MENTIONS KNITTING FOR THE HOME, AFGHANS AND CUSHION COVERS IMMEDIATELY COME TO MIND. To me, that's just the starting point for all the wonderful things you can create to add handmade touches to your home that are little pieces of your personality. My goal for this chapter is to provide you with quirky and interesting designs that will become a part of your everyday collection, as well as heirloom-worthy decoratives destined to be passed down to future generations. For the table, there are placemats (see page 110), *Op Art Graphic Coasters* (see page 102) and even flirty napkin skirts (see page 100). And the rug (see page 96), *Celebration Table Runner* (see page 88), doily (see page 108) and lacy mohair curtain (see page 112) in this chapter can be used to decorate any room in your home. I hope these projects will inspire you to create a more colorful way of living!

This afghan was influenced by the collage work of Dada husband-and-wife duo Hans Arp and Sophie Taeuber-Arp. Dada is an anti-art movement that began in Zurich, Switzerland, during World War I. Dadaists ignored prevailing aesthetics and cultural standards and sought to provoke the viewer to develop his or her own interpretation of the work presented. We have certainly entered a new age of knitting where the old rules need not apply. In the spirit of Dadaism, feel free to play around with the design and explore your own arrangement of colors.

dada
{ DENIM THROW }

CONSTRUCTION NOTES

This throw is knit in eleven separate strips, numbered from right to left. These yarns are meant to fade slightly with each wash, leaving a patina resembling your favorite pair of jeans. There is a slight shrinkage, so be sure to wash the yarn that you intend to use for seaming beforehand. If you would like to preserve the crisp look of your throw, opt for dry cleaning.

MEASUREMENTS
45" x 58" (114cm x 147cm)

YARN
6 skeins Rowan Denim (100% cotton 102 yds [93m] per 50g) in each of the foll colors:
  color #225 Nashville (A)
  color #229 Memphis (B)
  color #231 Tennessee (C)
  color #324 Ecru (D)

Or substitute 600 yds (548m) of dk weight cotton yarn for each color.

If necessary, change needle size to obtain correct gauge.

NEEDLES + NOTIONS
size US 6 (4mm) needles

If necessary, change needle size to obtain correct gauge.

tapestry needle

GAUGE
20 sts and 28 rows = 4" (10cm) in St st

DENIM THROW

STRIP 1
With C, cast on 16 sts.

Knit 4 rows.

BEGIN PATTERN

ROW 1 (RS): Knit.

ROW 2 (WS): K2, p10, k4.

Rep Rows 1–2 until piece measures 14½" (37cm), ending with a WS row.

Change to A and cont in est patt for 14½" (37cm), ending with a WS row.

Change to D and cont in est patt for 14½" (37cm), ending with a WS row.

Change to B and cont in est patt for 14¼" (36cm), ending with a WS row.

Knit 4 rows. Bind off.

STRIP 2
With A, cast on 16 sts.

Knit 4 rows.

BEGIN PATTERN

ROW 1 (RS): Knit.

ROW 2 (WS): K2, p12, k2.

Rep Rows 1–2 until piece measures 14½" (37cm), ending with a WS row.

Change to B and cont in est patt for 14½" (37cm), ending with a WS row.

Change to C and cont in est patt for 14½" (37cm), ending with a WS row.

Change to D and cont in est patt for 14¼" (36cm), ending with a WS row.

Knit 4 rows. Bind off.

STRIP 3
With D, cast on 32 sts.

Knit 4 rows.

BEGIN PATTERN

ROW 1 (RS): Knit.

ROW 2 (WS): K2, p28, k2.

Rep Rows 1–2 until piece measures 14½" (37cm), ending with a WS row.

Change to C and cont in est patt for 14½" (37cm), ending with a WS row.

Change to B and cont in est patt for 14½" (37cm), ending with a WS row.

Change to A and cont in est patt for 14¼" (36cm), ending with a WS row.

Knit 4 rows. Bind off.

STRIP 4
With B, cast on 16 sts.

Knit 4 rows.

BEGIN PATTERN

ROW 1 (RS): Knit.

ROW 2 (WS): K2, p12, k2.

Rep Rows 1–2 until piece measures 14½" (37cm), ending with a WS row.

Change to D and cont in est patt for 14½" (37cm), ending with a WS row.

Change to A and cont in est patt for 14½" (37cm), ending with a WS row.

Change to C and cont in est patt for 14¼" (36cm), ending with a WS row.

Knit 4 rows. Bind off.

STRIP 5
With A, cast on 16 sts.

Knit 4 rows.

BEGIN PATTERN

ROW 1 (RS): Knit.

ROW 2 (WS): K2, p12, k2.

Rep Rows 1–2 until piece measures 14½" (37cm), ending with a WS row.

Change to B and cont in est patt for 14½" (37cm), ending with a WS row.

Change to C and cont in est patt for 14½" (37cm), ending with a WS row.

Change to D and cont in est patt for 14½" (37cm), ending with a WS row.

Knit 4 rows. Bind off.

STRIP 6
With B, cast on 32 sts.

Knit 4 rows.

BEGIN PATTERN

ROW 1 (RS): Knit.

ROW 2 (WS): K2, p28, k2.

Rep Rows 1–2 until piece measures 14½" (37cm), ending with a WS row.

Change to D and cont in est patt for 14½" (37cm), ending with a WS row.

Change to A and cont in est patt for 14½" (37cm), ending with a WS row.

Change to C and cont in est patt for 14¼" (36cm), ending with a WS row.

Knit 4 rows. Bind off.

STRIP 7

With D, cast on 16 sts.

Knit 4 rows.

BEGIN PATTERN

ROW 1 (RS): Knit.

ROW 2 (WS): K2, p12, k2.

Rep Rows 1–2 until piece measures 14½" (37cm), ending with a WS row.

Change to C and cont in est patt for 14½" (37cm), ending with a WS row.

Change to B and cont in patt for 14½" (37cm), ending with a WS row.

Change to A and cont in patt for 14¼" (36cm), ending with a WS row.

Knit 4 rows. Bind off.

STRIP 8

With C, cast on 16 sts.

Knit 4 rows.

BEGIN PATTERN

ROW 1 (RS): Knit.

ROW 2 (WS): K2, p12, k2.

Rep Rows 1–2 until piece measures 14½" (37cm), ending with a WS row.

Change to A and cont in est patt for 14½" (37cm), ending with a WS row.

Change to D and cont in patt for 14½" (37cm), ending with a WS row.

Change to B and cont in patt for 14¼" (36cm), ending with a WS row.

Knit 4 rows. Bind off.

STRIP 9

With A, cast on 32 sts.

Knit 4 rows.

BEGIN PATTERN

ROW 1 (RS): Knit.

ROW 2 (WS): K2, p28, k2.

Rep Rows 1–2 until piece measures 14½" (37cm), ending with a WS row.

Change to B and cont in est patt for 14½" (37cm), ending with a WS row.

Change to C and cont in patt for 14½" (37cm), ending with a WS row.

Change to D and cont in patt for 14¼" (36cm), ending with a WS row.

Knit 4 rows. Bind off.

STRIP 10

With D, cast on 16 sts.

Knit 4 rows.

BEGIN PATTERN

ROW 1 (RS): Knit.

ROW 2 (WS): K2, p12, k2.

Rep Rows 1–2 until piece measures 14½" (37cm), ending with a WS row.

Change to C and cont in est patt for 14½" (37cm), ending with a WS row.

Change to B and cont in patt for 14½" (37cm), ending with a WS row.

Change to A and cont in patt for 14¼" (36cm), ending with a WS row.

Knit 4 rows. Bind off.

STRIP 11

With B, cast on 16 sts.

Knit 4 rows.

BEGIN PATTERN

ROW 1 (RS): Knit.

ROW 2 (WS): k4, p10, k2.

Rep Rows 1–2 until piece measures 14½" (37cm), ending with a WS row.

Change to D and cont in est patt for 14½" (37cm), ending with a WS row.

Change to A and cont in patt for 14½" (37cm), ending with a WS row.

Change to C and cont in patt for 14¼" (36cm), ending with a WS row.

Knit 4 rows. Bind off.

FINISHING

Seam strips together in order given, using mattress stitch. (See the Glossary, page 120, for instructions on working in mattress stitch.) Weave in ends.

The Hudson Cushion Cover *is sophisticated, and it has a slightly masculine feel,* making it the perfect accent for a chair in a library or a man's study. Its textured pattern, combined with earthy blues and greens, gives it an organic quality that lends itself well to a room designed for comfort and contemplation. Its simple design works well with any color combination. Go camo with olive, charcoal and khaki, or give it a more tropical feel with turquoise, orange and lime. The possibilities are endless!

hudson
{ CUSHION COVER }

CONSTRUCTION NOTES

The back and top flap of this cushion cover are knit in one piece. The front is knit separately, then the two sides are seamed together. The pillow is worked in double moss stitch, a simple knit-and-purl pattern repeated over four rows that creates a very rich texture.

MEASUREMENTS
16" x 16" (41cm x 41cm)

YARN
1 skein Rowan Scottish Tweed Aran (100% wool, 186 yds [170m]) per 100g) in each of the foll colors:

    color #002 Machair (A)
    color #031 Indigo (B)
    color #032 Lewis Blue (C)
    color #033 Lovat (D)

Or substitute 186 yds (170m) of any worsted weight wool yarn for each color.

NEEDLES + NOTIONS
size US 8 (5mm) needles

If necessary, change needle size to obtain correct gauge.

four ¾" (19mm) buttons

one 14" x 14" (36cm x 36cm) pillow insert

safety pins

tapestry needle

GAUGE
17 sts and 28 rows = 4" (10cm) in St st

DOUBLE MOSS STITCH
Worked over a multiple of 4 sts.

ROW 1: * K2, p2; rep from * to end.

ROW 2: * K2, p2; rep from * to end.

ROW 3: * P2, k2; rep from * to end.

ROW 4: * P2, k2; rep from * to end.

Rep Rows 1–4.

CUSHION COVER

BACK
With D, cast on 48 sts.

Knit 2 rows.

Note: The patt beg on a WS row.

Change to A and work in double moss st until piece measures 5¼" (13cm), ending with Row 2 or 4.

Knit 1 row.

Change to B and knit 1 row. Cont in double moss st, beg with Row 1, until piece measures 10¾" (27cm), ending with Row 2 or 4.

Knit 1 row.

Change to C and knit 1 row. Cont in double moss st, beg with Row 1, until piece measures 16" (41cm), ending with Row 2 or 4.

Change to D. Knit 2 rows. Bind off.

Turn panel sideways. With RS facing, using B, pick up and knit 68 sts across top of the 3 panels.

Knit 1 row.

Change to D. Knit 2 rows.

Cont in the foll patt until piece measures 16¼" (41cm), ending with Row 2 or 4:

ROW 1: K2, * k2, p2; rep from * to last 2 sts, k2.

ROW 2: K2, * k2, p2; rep from * to last 2 sts, k2.

ROW 3: K2, * p2, k2; rep from * to last 2 sts, k2.

ROW 4: K2, * p2, k2; rep from * to last 2 sts, k2.

Place a safety pin at the beg and end of the last row to mark end of side seam.

TOP FLAP

CHANGE TO A: Knit 2 rows.

CHANGE TO D: Knit 2 rows.

Cont in the foll patt until piece measures approx 23" (58cm), ending with Row 2 or 4:

ROW 1: K2, * k2, p2; rep from * to last 2 sts, k2.

ROW 2: K2, * k2, p2; rep from * to last 2 sts, k2.

ROW 3: K2, * p2, k2; rep from * to last 2 sts, k2.

ROW 4: K2, * p2, k2; rep from * to last 2 sts, k2.

Knit 2 rows.

BUTTONHOLE ROW (RS): K4, yo, k2tog, k17, k2tog, yo, k18, yo, k2tog, k17, k2tog, yo, k4.

Knit 1 row.

CHANGE TO C: Knit 2 rows.

CHANGE TO D: Knit 2 rows.

Change to B and bind off.

FRONT
With D, cast on 68 sts.

Knit 2 rows.

Note: The patt beg on a WS row.

Change to A and work in double moss st until piece measures 5¼" (13cm), ending with Row 2 or 4.

Knit 1 row.

Change to B and knit 1 row. Cont in double moss st, beg with Row 1, until piece measures 10¾" (27cm), ending with Row 2 or 4.

Knit 1 row.

Change to C and knit 1 row. Cont in double moss st, beg with Row 1, until piece measures 16" (41cm), ending with Row 2 or 4.

Change to D. Knit 2 rows. Bind off.

FINISHING
Sew side seams. Sew on buttons to align with buttonholes.

celebration
{ TABLE RUNNER }

I don't believe in saving precious things for special occasions. I always use my good china, and at every meal I set the table with my great-great-grandmother's silverware. I love the idea of making the act of dining a celebration. It is a simple way to show gratitude for all the blessings in your life. Whether used for a special occasion or for your daily meals, this lovely hemp table runner will bring a festive spirit to your table.

CONSTRUCTION NOTES

This pattern is designed to adorn a long dining table. However, it is easy to customize the runner to fit any table. Knit until ½" (1cm) less than your desired length, knit four rows, and then bind off.

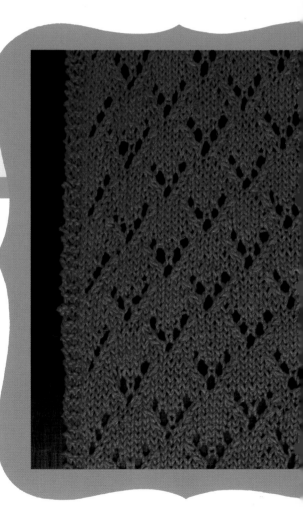

MEASUREMENTS
8½" x 63½" (22cm x 161cm)

YARN
3 skeins Lanaknits Allhemp6 (100% hemp, 165 yds [151m] per 100g)
    color Brick

Or substitute 450 yds (411m) of any dk weight hemp yarn.

NEEDLES + HOOKS
size US 5 (3.75mm) needles

If necessary, change needle size to obtain correct gauge.

size G (4mm or 4.5mm) crochet hook

GAUGE
18 sts and 32 rows = 4" (10cm) in patt on size US 5 (3.75mm) needles

TABLE RUNNER

Cast on 38 sts.

Knit 4 rows.

BEGIN PATTERN

ROW 1 (RS): K4, * yo, sl 1, k1, psso, k8; rep from * to last 4 sts, k4.

ROW 2 AND ALL WS ROWS: K3, purl to last 3 sts, k3.

ROW 3: K4, * k1, yo, sl 1, k1, psso, k5, k2tog, yo; rep from * to last 4 sts, k4.

ROW 5: K4, * k2, yo, sl 1, k1, psso, k3, k2tog, yo, k1; rep from * to last 4 sts, k4.

ROW 7: K4, * k5, yo, sl 1, k1, psso, k3; rep from * to last 4 sts, k4.

ROW 9: K4, * k3, k2tog, yo, k1, yo, sl 1, k1, psso, k2; rep from * to last 4 sts, k4.

ROW 11: K4, * k2, k2tog, yo, k3, yo, sl 1, k1, psso, k1; rep from * to last 4 sts, k4.

ROW 12: Rep Row 2.

Rep Rows 1–12 until piece measures approx 63" (160cm), ending with Row 11.

Knit 4 rows. Bind off.

FINISHING

KNOTTED FRINGE
Cut 42 19" (48cm) strands for fringe. Use 3 strands for each fringe, making 7 separate fringes for each side. Insert crochet hook through fabric, place doubled strands over hook and pull through. Draw ends through loop on hook and pull tightly. After making fringe across fabric, take one half of the strands from each fringe and knot them with half the strands from the next fringe.

Creating a sacred space for meditation provides a great support for your practice, as well as giving you a well-needed place to just relax and regroup. The area in your home where you meditate holds the energy you generate during meditation, as does the mat you sit on. As you knit this mat, repeat a favorite mantra or prayer, infusing it with the love and serenity you seek to attain from your meditative practice.

om
{ MEDITATION MAT }

CONSTRUCTION NOTES

This is a great stash-busting project! Break out your leftover skeins and bits of yarn, and design a color arrangement that speaks to you. Use this design as a template, making your own mat smaller or larger by stopping short of the number of repeats listed or by continuing on until you have reached your desired size. Use your imagination when deciding when and where to change colors around the border.

MEASUREMENTS
approx 26" x 20" (66cm x 51cm)

YARN
1 skein Lion Brand Fishermen's Wool (100% pure virgin wool, 465 yds [425m] per 226g), working with 2 strands held tog
> color #098 Natural (MC)

Or substitute 425 yds (388m) of any worsted weight wool.

approx 450 yds [411 m] of any bulky weight wool for the border
> 1 or more color(s) of your choice (CC)

Or substitute 2 strands of worsted weight wool held tog.

NEEDLES + NOTIONS
24" to 29" (61cm to 74cm) size US 10½ (6.5mm) circular needle

If necessary, change needle size to obtain correct gauge.

several stitch holders or spare circular needles

tapestry needles

GAUGE
14 sts and 22 rows = 4" (10cm) in St st with 2 strands of MC held tog

MEDITATION MAT

CENTER

Using 2 strands of MC, cast on 77 sts. Knit 2 rows.

BEGIN PATTERN

ROW 1: Knit.

ROW 2: K2, purl until last 2 sts, p2.

Rep Rows 1–2 until piece measures 16¾" (42cm), ending with Row 1.

Knit 1 row. Bind off.

BORDER

With CC and RS facing, pick up and knit 51 sts along side A. (See the Glossary, page 120, for instructions on picking up sts.) Turn work and knit 1 row. Cut yarn. Put sts on stitch holders or on a spare circular needle.

Beg at end of picked up sts on side A, using CC, with RS facing pick up and knit 77 sts across side B (1 st from end of side A and 76 sts across side B.) Turn work and knit 1 row. Cut yarn. Put sts on stitch holders or on a spare circular needle.

Beg at end of picked up sts on side B, using CC, with RS facing, pick up and knit 52 sts across side C (1 st from end of side B and 51 sts across side C). Turn work and knit 1 row. Cut yarn. Put sts on stitch holders or on a spare circular needle.

Beg at end of picked up sts on side C, using CC, with RS facing, pick up and knit 78 sts across side D (1 st from end of side C, 76 across side D, 1 from side A). Turn work and knit 1 row. Cut yarn. Put sts on stitch holders or on a spare circular needle.

Cont to work the border in this fashion, picking up 1 st at beg, knitting sts from holder or spare needle, then picking up 1 st at end. Turn work, knit 1 row and then cont on to the next side.

On the 6th repetition, after the knit row, bind off.

FINISHING

Seam corners.

Om Meditation Mat *Diagram*

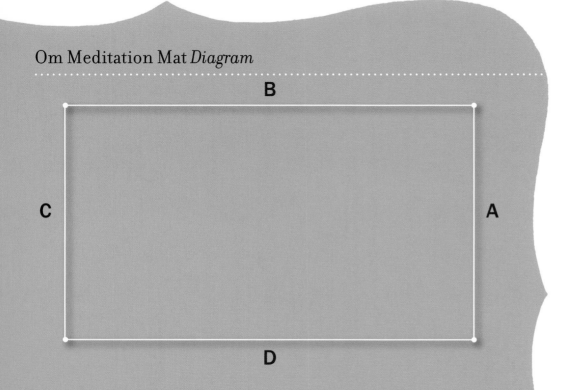

veracruz
{ KITCHEN RUG }

Brightly colored accessories always remind me of sunny, tropical locales. They lift the spirits and bring a sense of fun and playfulness to a room. While I designed this as a kitchen rug, you can use it in any room in your house that needs a jolt of color! It is sturdy enough to work in a kid's playroom or in an interior entryway.

CONSTRUCTION NOTES

Due to the weight of the fabric, the C sections are knit in two parts and then seamed together down the middle.

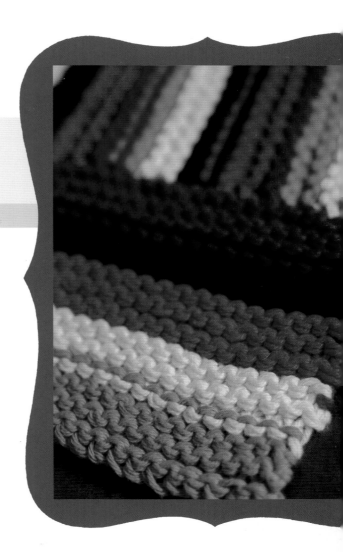

MEASUREMENTS
46" x 24" (117cm x 61cm)

YARN
2 skeins Lion Brand Lion Cotton (100% cotton, 236 yds [212m] per 113g) in each of the foll colors:

- color #157 Sunflower (A)
- color #110 Navy (B)
- color #112 Poppy Red (C)
- color #108 Morning Glory Blue (D)
- color #148 Turquoise (E)

Or substitute 472 yds (431m) of any worsted weight cotton yarn for each color.

NEEDLES + NOTIONS
32" to 40" (80cm to 100cm) size US 10½ (6.5mm) circular needle

If necessary, change needle size to obtain correct gauge.

safety pin or removable marker

tapestry needle

GAUGE
14 sts and 26 rows = 4" (10cm) in garter st wtih 2 strands held tog

KITCHEN RUG

You will be working with 2 strands of yarn held tog throughout patt.

SECTION A (CENTER RECTANGLE)

With A, cast on 89 sts. Work in garter st for 20 rows.

CHANGE TO B: Work in garter st for 9 rows.

CHANGE TO C: Work in garter st for 20 rows.

CHANGE TO D: Work in garter st for 9 rows.

CHANGE TO E: Work in garter st for 20 rows.

Bind off.

SECTION B (RECTANGLES AT NARROW ENDS OF SECTION A)

With RS facing, using C, pick up and knit 49 sts across narrow end of Section A. (See the Glossary, page 120, for instructions on picking up sts.)

Knit 3 rows.

CHANGE TO D: Knit 3 rows.

CHANGE TO E: Knit 4 rows.

CHANGE TO A: Knit 3 rows.

CHANGE TO B: Knit 4 rows.

*CHANGE TO C: Knit 3 rows.

CHANGE TO D: Knit 4 rows.

CHANGE TO E: Knit 3 rows.

CHANGE TO A: Knit 4 rows.

CHANGE TO B: Knit 3 rows.

CHANGE TO C: Knit 4 rows.

CHANGE TO D: Knit 3 rows.

CHANGE TO E: Knit 4 rows.

CHANGE TO A: Knit 3 rows.

CHANGE TO B: Knit 4 rows.

Rep from *, if necessary, until Section B measures approx 8½" (22cm).

Bind off.

Rep Section B at opposite end of Section A.

SECTION C (RECTANGLES ON LONG SIDES OF SECTIONS A/B)

Due to the weight and length of the rug, this section will be worked in 2 parts on each side and then seamed tog.

Using a marker or safety pin, mark the center of Section A. Beg at top right corner of Section B and cont across to the marker, with RS facing and using D, pick up and knit 74 sts.

Knit 5 rows. At the end of the fifth row (WS), do not turn work, but slide sts back to other end of needle. Change to B and knit 1 WS row. (You have just knit two WS rows in succession. This is the only place in the patt where this occurs. For the rest of the patt, cont working garter st in the normal fashion.)

Knit 4 more rows with B.

CHANGE TO C: Knit 6 rows.

CHANGE TO A: Knit 5 rows.

CHANGE TO E: Knit 6 rows.

Bind off.

Working from center marker to top left corner of Section B, with RS facing, pick up and knit 74 sts and rep Section C using the foll color sequence: B, D, C, E, A. Rep on the opposite side.

FINISHING

Using mattress stitch, sew center seam of Section C on each side. (See the Glossary, page 120, for instructions on working mattress stitch.)

Veracruz Kitchen Rug *Diagram*

	C		C	
B		A		B
	C		C	

To me, the mark of a great host is that he or she has lovingly attended to even the smallest details of presentation. It shows your guests that you find entertaining a pleasure and not a chore. Whether you are planning a backyard barbecue or a more formal affair, these lovely little napkin skirts are a delicious way to bring a bit of pizzazz to your next celebratory occasion.

flirt
{ NAPKIN SKIRT }

CONSTRUCTION NOTES

Making a buttonhole is about as complicated as this pattern gets! You can keep your skirts sweet and simple with plain buttons or dress them up with something more ornate.

MEASUREMENTS

3½" x 3¾" (9cm x 10cm)

YARN

1 skein Lanaknits Allhemp3 (100% hemp, 165 yds [150m] per 50g)

colors Lilac and Sprout shown

Or substitute 165 yds (150m) of any fingering- or sport-weight hemp yarn.

1 skein makes enough Napkin Skirts for an intimate dinner party (about 6).

NEEDLES + NOTIONS

size US 2 (2.75mm) needles

If necessary, change needle size to obtain correct gauge.

two ⅜" (10mm) buttons

GAUGE

26 sts and 40 rows = 4" (10cm) in St st

NAPKIN SKIRT

Cast on 50 sts.

Work in St st for 1" (3cm), ending with a purl row.

NEXT ROW: K2tog across—25 sts.

Purl 1 row.

Knit 7 rows.

NEXT ROW: K3, purl to last 3 sts, k3.

BUTTONHOLE ROW (RS): K2, k2tog, yo twice, k2tog, knit to end of row.

NEXT ROW (WS): K3, purl to last 3 sts, k3.

NEXT ROW (RS): Knit.

Rep last 2 rows until piece measures 3½" (9cm) from cast-on edge, ending with WS row.

Rep Buttonhole Row.

NEXT ROW: K3, purl to last 3 sts, k3.

Knit 6 rows. Bind off.

FINISHING

Sew on buttons. Weave in any ends.

When I was a kid, I was fascinated with optical art.
I would make myself sick watching those dizzying images as they
appeared to sway and pulsate. Putting two strong, contrasting
colors together can create the same mesmerizing appearance of
vibration and movement. This fast and fun project is a painless
introduction to intarsia knitting.

op art
{ GRAPHIC COASTERS }

CONSTRUCTION NOTES

Intarsia charts are read from right to left on odd-numbered rows and from left to right
on even-numbered rows. Usually all the stitches on odd-numbered rows are knit and on
even-numbered rows they are purled. However, for this design you will knit the first and last
stitch on every row to make a garter stitch border.

MEASUREMENTS
4½" x 4½" (11cm x 11cm)

YARN
1 skein Lion Brand Lion Cotton (100%
cotton, 236 yds [216m] per 113g) in
each of the foll colors:
>   color #112 Poppy Red (A)
>   color #108 Morning Glory Blue (B)

*Or substitute 236 yds (216m) of
any worsted weight cotton yarn
for each color.*

*2 skeins makes enough coasters
for a family reunion (around 24).*

NEEDLES + HOOKS
size US 7 (4.5mm) needles

*If necessary, change needle size
to obtain correct gauge.*

size G (4.25mm) crochet hook

GAUGE
18 sts and 28 rows =
4" (10cm) in St st on size
US 7 (4.5mm) needles

GRAPHIC COASTERS

Cast on 18 sts. Knit 3 rows (Rows
1–3 of chart).

NEXT ROW: K1, purl to last st, k1 (Row
4 of chart).

Cont knitting chart as shown, knitting
1 st at the beg and end of every row
(Rows 5–24 of chart).

Knit 2 rows (Rows 25–26 of chart).
Bind off.

FINISHING
Using the same color yarn as in the
center of the design, work 1 rnd of
single crochet around the edges. (See
the Glossary, page 118, for instructions on working in single crochet.)

KEY
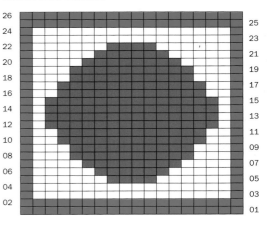

■ = CC: Knit on odd rows, purl on even rows

□ = MC: Knit on odd rows, purl on even rows

■ = MC: Knit on both odd and even rows

COASTER CHART

metropolis

{ STRIPED BLOCKS THROW }

As a child, I spent a lot of time sitting on my front steps and observing life around me. I can still remember the sounds, the scents and especially the colors of my childhood. Depending upon the time of day, the buildings took on various shades of pink, red and brown. For this throw, I chose colors that are reminiscent of the brownstones and brick row houses of my youth. The *Metropolis* afghan is a super-easy project with a sophisticated look.

CONSTRUCTION NOTES

This afghan is knit in five horizontal strips worked from side to side. Knit it as pictured or knit each strip with a different colored yarn from your stash, giving it a totally unique look—you might use colors that remind you of your own childhood.

MEASUREMENTS
40" x 48" (102cm x 122cm)

YARN
2 skeins of Peace Fleece Worsted (wool/mohair blend, 200 yds [183m] per 113g) in each of the foll colors:

> *color Moldova Burgundy (A)*
> *color Buffalo Brownski (B)*
> *color Samantha/Katya Pink (C)*
> *color Ancient Fern (D)*
> *color Georgia Rose (E)*

Or substitute 275 yds (251m) of any worsted weight wool for each color listed above.

NEEDLES + NOTIONS
size US 9 (5.5mm) needles

If necessary, change needle size to obtain correct gauge.

tapestry needle

GAUGE
15 sts and 24 rows = 4" (10cm) in St st

STRIPED BLOCKS THROW

STRIP 1
With A, cast on 38 sts.

Knit 6 rows.

BEGIN PATTERN

ROW 1 (RS): Knit.

ROW 2 (WS): K5, purl to end of row.

Rep the last 2 rows 4 times (10 rows).

Cont in est patt, knitting the first 5 sts of each WS row, as you work the foll color sequence:

CHANGE TO B: Work 16 rows.

CHANGE TO C: Work 16 rows.

CHANGE TO D: Work 16 rows.

CHANGE TO E: Work 16 rows.

CHANGE TO A: Work 16 rows.

CHANGE TO B: Work 16 rows.

CHANGE TO C: Work 16 rows.

CHANGE TO D: Work 16 rows.

CHANGE TO E: Work 16 rows.

CHANGE TO A: Work 16 rows.

CHANGE TO B: Work 16 rows.

CHANGE TO C: Work 16 rows.

CHANGE TO D: Work 16 rows.

CHANGE TO E: Work 10 rows.

Knit 6 rows. Bind off.

STRIPS 2 + 4
With C, cast on 38 sts.

Knit 7 rows. Purl 1 row (WS).

Work in St st as you work the foll color sequence:

CHANGE TO D: Work 16 rows.

CHANGE TO E: Work 16 rows.

CHANGE TO A: Work 16 rows.

CHANGE TO B: Work 16 rows.

CHANGE TO C: Work 16 rows.

CHANGE TO D: Work 16 rows.

CHANGE TO E: Work 16 rows.

CHANGE TO A: Work 16 rows.

CHANGE TO B: Work 16 rows.

CHANGE TO C: Work 16 rows.

CHANGE TO D: Work 16 rows.

CHANGE TO E: Work 16 rows.

CHANGE TO A: Work 16 rows.

CHANGE TO B: Work 16 rows.

Change to C. Knit 1 row, then purl 1 row. Knit 6 rows. Bind off.

STRIP 3
With A, cast on 38 sts.

Knit 6 rows.

Work 10 rows in St st, beg with a knit row.

Work in St st as you work the foll color sequence:

CHANGE TO B: Work 16 rows.

CHANGE TO C: Work 16 rows.

CHANGE TO D: Work 16 rows.

CHANGE TO E: Work 16 rows.

CHANGE TO A: Work 16 rows.

CHANGE TO B: Work 16 rows.

CHANGE TO C: Work 16 rows.

CHANGE TO D: Work 16 rows.

CHANGE TO E: Work 16 rows.

CHANGE TO A: Work 16 rows.

CHANGE TO B: Work 16 rows.

CHANGE TO C: Work 16 rows.

CHANGE TO D: Work 16 rows.

Change to E and cont in St st for 10 rows. Knit 6 rows. Bind off.

STRIP 5

With A, cast on 38 sts.

Knit 6 rows.

BEGIN PATTERN

ROW 1 (RS): Knit.

ROW 2 (WS): Purl to last 5 sts, k5.

Rep the last 2 rows 4 times (10 rows).

Cont in est patt, knitting the last 5 sts of each WS row, as you work the foll color sequence:

CHANGE TO B: Work 16 rows.

CHANGE TO C: Work 16 rows.

CHANGE TO D: Work 16 rows.

CHANGE TO E: Work 16 rows.

CHANGE TO A: Work 16 rows.

CHANGE TO B: Work 16 rows.

CHANGE TO C: Work 16 rows.

CHANGE TO D: Work 16 rows.

CHANGE TO E: Work 16 rows.

CHANGE TO A: Work 16 rows.

CHANGE TO B: Work 16 rows.

CHANGE TO C: Work 16 rows.

CHANGE TO D: Work 16 rows.

CHANGE TO E: Work 10 rows.

Knit 6 rows. Bind off.

FINISHING

Block strips. Sew tog using mattress stitch. (See the Glossary, page 120, for instructions on how to work mattress stitch.) Weave in any ends.

One can hardly hear the word doily without the image of a fragile, yellowed piece of lace languishing on a dusty old sofa coming to mind. It is time to reclaim the doily! Bring it into the twenty-first century by refashioning it with bold, sumptuous yarn and a modern stitch pattern. You can use this darling piece of fabric to cover a nightstand or end table or to adorn a home altar.

darling
{ MODERN DOILY }

CONSTRUCTION NOTES
This simple project is knit in one piece with a single skein of yarn, which means no finishing! If you are a novice knitter this is the perfect project on which to try your hand at knitting lace.

MEASUREMENTS
18¼" x 12" (46cm x 30cm)

YARN
1 skein Lorna's Laces Lion and Lamb (silk/wool blend, 205 yds [187m] per 100g)
  color Pine

Or substitute 205 yds (187m) of any worsted weight yarn.

NEEDLES
size US 9 (5.5mm) needles

If necessary, change needle size to obtain correct gauge.

GAUGE
20 sts and 27 rows = 4" (10cm) in patt

MODERN DOILY
Cast on 57 sts.

ROW 1: K1, * p1, k1; rep from * to end of row.

Rep Row 1 thrice.

BEGIN PATTERN

ROW 1 (RS): K1, (p1, k1) twice, knit to last 4 sts, (p1, k1) twice.

ROW 2 AND ALL WS ROWS: K1, (p1, k1) twice, purl to last 5 sts, k1, (p1, k1) twice.

ROW 3: K1, (p1, k1) twice, k1, * k2tog, yo, k2; rep from * to last 7 sts, k3, (p1, k1) twice.

ROW 5: Rep Row 1.

ROW 7: K1, (p1, k1) twice, k1, * k2, SSK, yo; rep from * to last 7 sts, k3, (p1, k1) twice.

ROW 8: Rep Row 2.

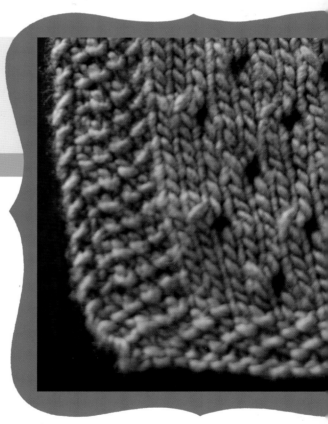

Rep Rows 1–8 until piece measures approx 17¾" (45cm), ending with Row 1 or Row 5.

NEXT ROW: K1, * p1, k1; rep from * to end of row.

Rep last row 3 times. Bind off. Weave in any ends.

rustic { **PLACEMAT** }

No matter what the occasion for your meal, the placemat would do well to avoid upstaging the china and the flatware! Ideally, it acts as a backdrop for the meal that is being served, subtly complementing all the elements on the table. The *Rustic Placemat* combines two elements I love—ease and casual elegance. Even the novice knitter will feel confident taking on this effortless project.

CONSTRUCTION NOTES

This super-easy project is knit in one piece, changing colors at the middle.

MEASUREMENTS
18" x 12" (46cm x 30cm)

YARN
1 skein of Lanaknits Allhemp6 (100% hemp, 165 yds [151m] per 100g) in each of the foll colors:

    color Avocado (A)
    color Sprout (B)

Or substitute 300 yds (229m) of any worsted weight yarn.

3 skeins of each color makes a set of 4 placemats.

NEEDLES + HOOKS
size US 4 (3.5mm) needles

If necessary, change needle size to obtain correct gauge.

size E (3.5mm) crochet hook

GAUGE
18 sts and 36 rows = 4" (10cm) in garter st on size US 4 (3.5mm) needles

PLACEMAT
With A, cast on 54 sts. Work in garter st until piece measures 9" (23cm), ending with a WS row.

Change to B and cont in garter st until piece measures 18" (46cm) from cast-on edge, ending with a WS row.

Bind off.

FINISHING
Work 1 rnd of single crochet around edges, working in color A on the half worked in color B, and vice versa. (See the Glossary, page 118, for instructions on working in single crochet.)

I am not easily seduced by the obviously expensive sofa or by precious objets d'art *that are meant to impress.* My eye is immediately drawn to the quirky and unexpected decor elements that give a room a shot of personality. I am even more thrilled when a common, everyday object is created with surprising materials or an uncommon design. With these things in mind, I designed the *Chain Maille Mohair Curtain*. This curtain is perfect for the awkward, tiny window that is difficult to dress. Or it can be cleverly displayed on a larger window between two sheer panels.

chain maille
{ MOHAIR CURTAIN }

CONSTRUCTION NOTES

The curtain rod pocket is knit with smaller needles, and the body is knit with larger needles. The weight of this fabric will cause your curtain to slowly lengthen over time.

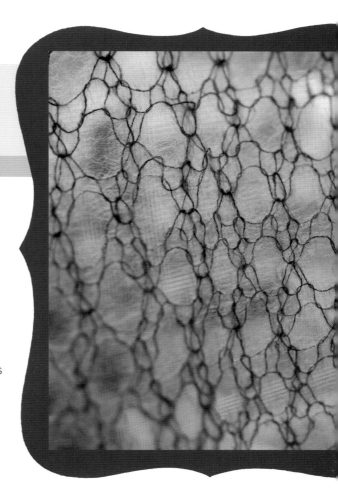

MEASUREMENTS
30" x 30" (76cm x 76cm)

YARN
2 skeins Rowan Kidsilk Night (mohair/silk blend, 227 yds [207m] per 25g)
  color #613 Oberon

Or substitute 365 yds (334m) of any lightweight yarn.

NEEDLES + NOTIONS
size US 8 (5mm) needles

size US 13 (9mm) needles

If necessary, change needle size to obtain correct gauge.

tapestry needle

GAUGE
18 sts and 24 rows = 4" (10cm) in St st on size US 8 (5mm) needles

9 sts and 16 rows = 4" (10cm) in patt on size US 13 (9mm) needles

MOHAIR CURTAIN

With size US 8 (5mm) needles, cast on 108 sts. Beg with a knit row, work in St st for 19 rows.

(WS) Knit 1 row for turning ridge.

(RS) Beg with a knit row, cont in St st for 19 rows, working the sts very loosely on the final row.

Change to size US 13 (9mm) needles.

DEC ROW: * K2, k2tog; rep from * to end of row—81 sts.

BEGIN PATTERN

ROW 1: K3, * yo, sl 1, k1, psso; rep from * to last 3 sts, k3.

ROWS 2–3: Knit.

Rep Rows 1–3 until piece measures 32" (81cm) from cast-on edge (or desired length plus 2" [5cm]), ending with Row 3.

Knit 3 rows. Bind off loosely.

FINISHING

Fold rod pocket hem to WS on turning ridge. With yarn threaded on a tapestry needle, slip st in place.

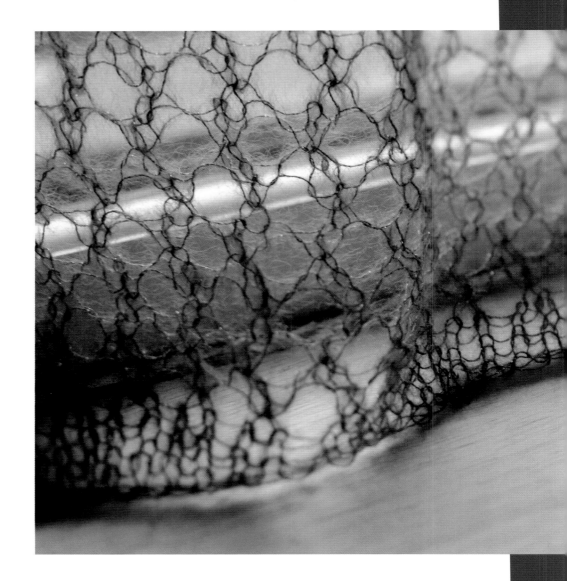

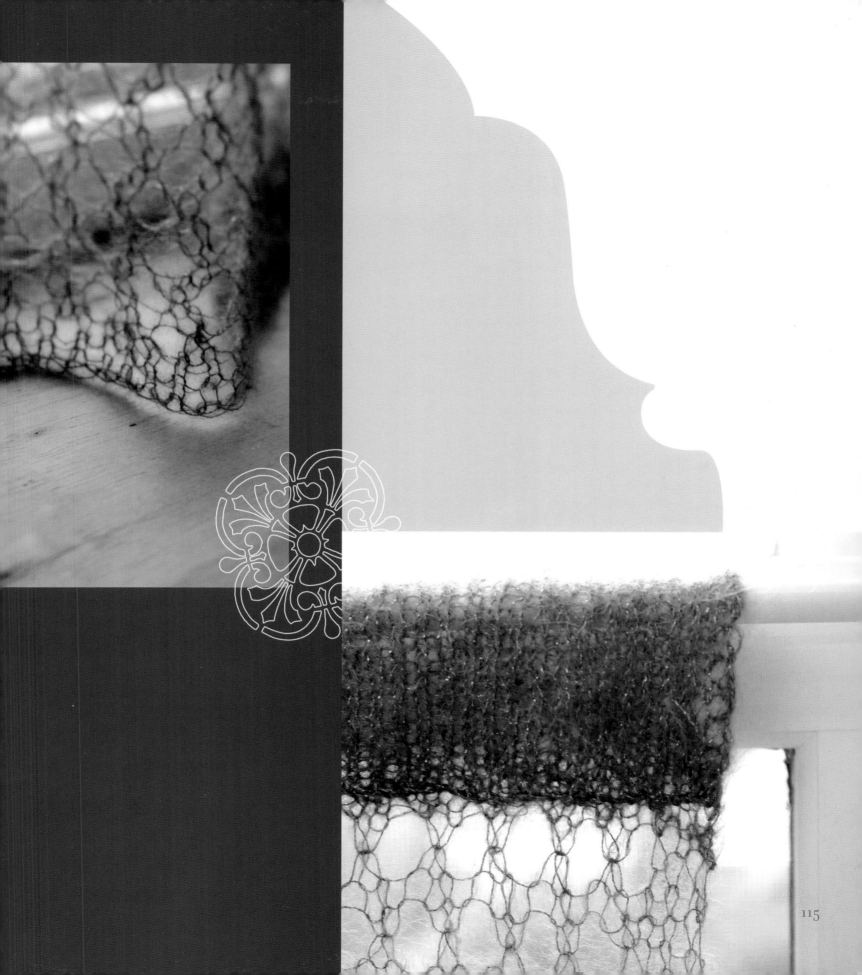

helpful INFORMATION

KNITTING ABBREVIATIONS

alt	ALTERNATE
beg	BEGINNING
BO	BIND OFF
CO	CAST ON
CC	CONTRAST COLOR
dec	DECREASE
DPN(s)	DOUBLE-POINTED NEEDLE(S)
est patt	ESTABLISHED PATTERN
foll	FOLLOWING
inc	INCREASE
k	KNIT
k2tog	KNIT 2 TOGETHER
MC	MAIN COLOR
p	PURL
p2tog	PURL 2 TOGETHER
p3tog	PURL 3 TOGETHER
pm	PLACE MARKER
psso	PASS SLIPPED STITCH OVER
rem	REMAINING
RS	RIGHT SIDE
rep	REPEAT
sl	SLIP
SSK	SLIP, SLIP, KNIT
st(s)	STITCH(ES)
WS	WRONG SIDE
yds	YARDS
yo	YARN OVER

KNITTING NEEDLE CONVERSIONS

diameter (mm)	US size	suggested yarn weight
2	0	LACE WEIGHT
2.25	1	LACE AND FINGERING WEIGHT
2.75	2	LACE AND FINGERING WEIGHT
3.25	3	FINGERING AND SPORT WEIGHT
3.5	4	FINGERING AND SPORT WEIGHT
3.75	5	DK AND SPORT WEIGHT
4	6	DK, SPORT AND ARAN/WORSTED WEIGHT
4.5	7	ARAN/WORSTED WEIGHT
5	8	ARAN/WORSTED AND HEAVY WORSTED WEIGHT
5.5	9	ARAN/WORSTED, HEAVY WORSTED
6	10	CHUNKY/BULKY
6.5	10½	CHUNKY/BULKY AND SUPER BULKY
8	11	CHUNKY/BULKY AND SUPER BULKY
9	13	SUPER BULKY
10	15	SUPER BULKY
12.75	17	SUPER BULKY
15	19	SUPER BULKY
36		SUPER BULKY

SUBSTITUTING YARNS

At the time of publication, all of the yarns used in this book were still being produced. However, a yarn company may decide to discontinue a particular yarn or color with little or no notice.

When it comes to substituting yarns, gauge is everything. Check the label to make sure that the horizontal gauge (number of stitches per inch) is the same as the required gauge in the pattern that you are working with. It is best to purchase all of the yarn at once, as it may be difficult to match your dye lot at a later date. Because every knitter knits in a different way, it is always necessary to knit a swatch to determine that you are getting the proper gauge, thus ensuring that the final measurements of your project will be as specified.

CARING FOR YOUR HANDKNITS

HAND-WASHING AND BLOCKING

Handknits should be soaked in cool water with a mild soap. Gently wring and then place on a dry towel and roll out the excess water. Transfer to a dry towel and lay flat to dry. Unless your aim is to stretch your item, you should never hang it to dry. If you are blocking your project to attain a certain measurement, you should pin it to the towel using rust-proof pins. I like to set a fan in front of my blocked project so it dries quicker. Heavy wools take a long time to dry, and if you live in a humid climate they will take even longer. Be sure to change the towel every twelve hours or so on long-drying projects. If your project remains wet for too long, it will begin to smell like laundry that has been left behind in the washer.

STORING YOUR HANDKNITS

Always clean your handknits before storing them, as moths tend to prefer dirty woolens, especially those with food stains. I stopped using mothballs when I discovered that they contain chemicals that can be hazardous to your health. Try storing your handknits with an herb sachet made of lavender, rosemary, cloves or other pungent herbs. Cedar balls and shavings are good, too, but need to be shaved or replaced when they've lost their scent. It is rumored that the solvent used in dry cleaning helps to prevent moths. If you opt to dry clean your projects, you should stick with that. Jumping back and forth between washing and dry cleaning is a no-no, as this tends to break down the fibers, reducing the life of your handknits.

EEK! A MOTH!

If you notice the fibers starting to unravel, chances are a moth has had its way with your stash or your handknits. Place the affected yarn or project in a plastic bag and toss it in the freezer for a day or so. This will kill off any moth larvae and prevent it from doing further damage. I have heard that the microwave also works (minus the plastic bag), but I find the idea a little frightening.

CARE SYMBOLS

Yarn labels can sometimes look like Greek. Here's a quick guide to the symbols you should know the meanings of so you can take good care of your handknits.

Do not wash by hand or machine

Hand washable

Do not press

Machine washable

Do not dry clean

GLOSSARY
knitting and crochet
terms and techniques

CASTING ON (CO)

Casting on is the term for creating the number of stitches needed for the first row of any project. There are several methods for casting on—for the projects in this book, you may use the method you're most comfortable with.

CROCHET STITCHES

Some projects in this book use a small crocheted border as a finishing technique. You don't need to know much about crochet; just knowing these basic stitches will do.

SLIP STITCH CROCHET

On right side of fabric, with edge facing away from you, insert hook into top edge of stitch, wrap yarn over hook and pull through fabric. * Insert hook into next stitch, wrap yarn over hook, pull through the fabric and through the loop on hook. Rep from * to create a border as desired.

SINGLE CROCHET

On right side of fabric, with edge facing away from you, insert hook into top edge of stitch, wrap yarn over hook and pull through fabric, wrap yarn over hook and pull through loop. * Insert hook into next stitch, wrap yarn over hook and pull through both loops on hook. Rep from * as desired.

DECREASES

Decreasing is one of the simplest knitting operations to learn. For the projects in this book, decreases are managed by knitting multiple stitches together as one.

KNIT TWO TOGETHER (K2TOG)

Knitting two stitches together as one (k2tog) is a simple way to decrease the number of stitches in a row. Simply slip your right-hand needle through the first two stitches on the left-hand needle, as for a regular knit stitch. Knit the two stitches as one, creating one less stitch.

PURL TWO TOGETHER (P2TOG)

Slip your right-hand needle through the first two stitches on the left-hand needle, as for a regular purl stitch. Purl the two stitches as one, creating one less stitch.

PURL THREE TOGETHER (P3TOG)

Slip your right-hand needle through the first three stitches on the left-hand needle, as for a regular purl stitch. Purl the three stitches as one, decreasing by two stitches.

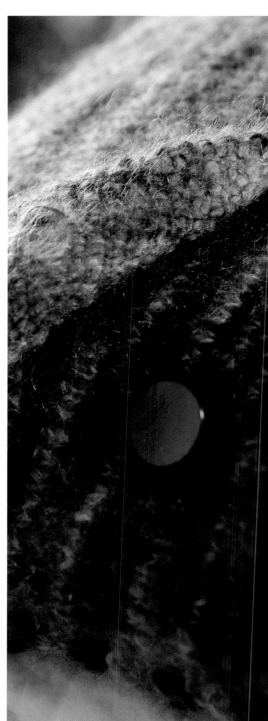

INCREASES

There are lots of different ways to increase the number of stitches in a given row. If the pattern simply says inc 1, choose the method of increasing that works best for you.

KNIT ONE IN FRONT AND BACK (KFB)

An easy way to increase is to knit one in the front and back of a stitch (kfb). To make this type of increase, simply insert your right-hand needle into the next stitch on the left-hand needle and knit the stitch, keeping the stitch on the left-hand needle instead of sliding it off. Then bring your right-hand needle around to the back, knit into the back loop of the same stitch, and slip both stitches off the needle. (See Knit One in Front and Back, Fig 1–3.)

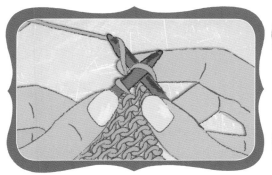

Knit One in Front and Back: Fig 1

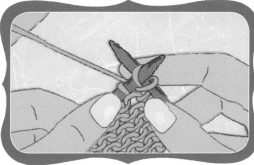

Knit One in Front and Back: Fig 2

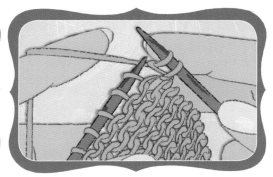

Knit One in Front and Back: Fig 3

MAKE ONE (M1)

With your right-hand needle, pick up the bar between two stitches from the back to front, and place it on the left-hand needle, then knit it through the back loop. (See Make One, Fig 1–2.)

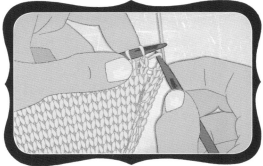

Make One: Fig 1

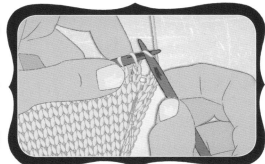

Make One: Fig 2

INTARSIA

At each color change, yarns must be wrapped around each other at the back of the work to prevent holes in the fabric. You may work with separate skeins, with yarn wound on bobbins, or with very long strands of yarn. Take time to untangle your strands every few rows.

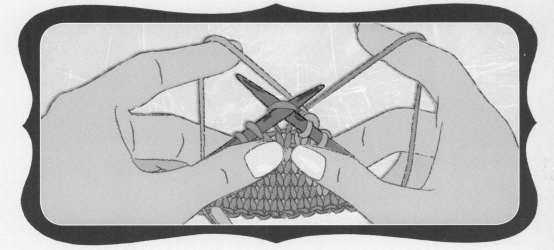

Intarsia

GLOSSARY

continued

MATTRESS STITCH

Unless otherwise indicated, mattress stitch is used for all seams in this book. Mattress stitch creates an invisible seam by replicating the stitches on either side of the seam using a darning needle and the same yarn used to create the knitted piece.

To create mattress stitch on stockinette pieces, work on the right side of the fabric, bringing the needle up between the two legs of a v stitch on one piece, down through the front of the fabric outside of the v stitch on the other piece of fabric, under both legs of the same stitch, up through the fabric on the other outside of that same stitch, then down through the right side of the first piece of fabric at the same point where you brought the needle up for the first part of the stitch. Repeat along the entire length of the seam. See a reference guide for working mattress stitch on garter stitch. (See Mattress Stitch, Fig 1–4.)

Picking Up Stitches

PICKING UP STITCHES

To pick up a stitch, insert the tip of one needle through the side of a stitch from front to back. Leaving about a 3" to 4" (8cm to 10cm) tail, wrap the yarn around the needle as you would for a regular knit stitch. Bring the yarn through the stitch, creating a loop on your needle. This loop is the first picked-up stitch. Continue to pick up the number of stitches required, making sure to space them evenly.

PLACING A MARKER (PM)

Sometimes a pattern calls for you to place a marker (pm). Markers are generally small plastic rings that slide onto a needle and rest in between stitches, marking a certain spot. If you don't have markers on hand, cut small pieces of scrap yarn in a contrasting color. Tie the scrap yarn around the needle in the indicated spot in a loose knot. Move the marker from one needle to the other when you come to it. Continue as usual.

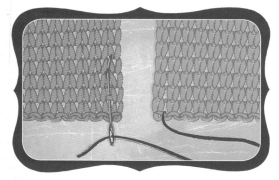

Mattress Stitch: Fig 1

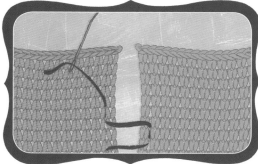

Mattress Stitch: Fig 2

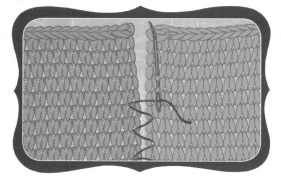

Mattress Stitch: Fig 3

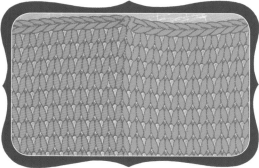

Mattress Stitch: Fig 4

STITCHES

EYELETS

Eyelets are small, decorative holes in knitted fabric. Create them with regular yarn overs. Remember to make an equal number of decreases on the following row so the knitted fabric doesn't grow exponentially.

GARTER STITCH

Garter stitch is created by knitting every row.

RIBBING

To create ribbing, simply alternate between knitting and purling. You can create a one-by-one rib, a two-by-two rib, a one-by-three rib...etc. Ribbing is often used as a border or as trim.

SEED STITCH

Seed stitch is a simple stitch that creates an interesting texture. Seed stitch is worked by knitting all purl stitches and purling all knit stitches. Here's how it works:

FOR AN ODD NUMBER OF STITCHES

ROW 1: * k1, p1; rep from * until last st, k1.

Rep Row 1.

FOR AN EVEN NUMBER OF STITCHES

ROW 1: * k1, p1*, rep from * until end of row.

ROW 2: * p1, k1; rep from * until end of row.

Rep Rows 1–2.

STOCKINETTE STITCH

To create Stockinette stitch, knit on the right side and purl on the wrong side. If you're knitting in the round, knitting every row produces effortless Stockinette with no purling.

YARN OVER (YO)

A yarn over is as easy as it sounds. When you come to a yarn over in the pattern, simply wrap the working yarn around the right-hand needle and continue knitting as usual. On the following row, you will knit or purl the wrapped yarn, creating an extra stitch and also an attractive eyelet hole in the knitted fabric. Because a yarn over creates a new stitch, a row with yarn overs is often combined with decreases.

WHIP STITCH

Fold, at the turning ridge, to the wrong side, lining the edges up evenly. Starting at the corner edge, insert the tapestry needle into a stitch on the wrong side of the fabric and then into the cast-on edge of the fabric that is folded over, and pull the yarn through. Repeat until the end.

WORKING IN THE ROUND

WITH CIRCULAR NEEDLES

Before you begin, make sure that your circular needles are a bit shorter than the diameter of your project. Simply cast on the requisite number of stitches just as you would on straight needles. Also make sure the stitches are not twisted. Hold the needle with the tail dangling from it in your left hand. Push the stitches to the end of the needle. Hold the needle with the working yarn in your right hand, pushing the first stitches to the end of that needle. Insert the tip of the right needle into the first stitch on the left needle from front to back. Wrap the working yarn around the right needle and knit your first stitch. Voilá, you're connected! After that, knit every row to produce Stockinette stitch.

WITH DOUBLE-POINTED NEEDLES

If one of your double-pointed needles can accommodate the full number of stitches, cast all of the stitches onto one needle. If your needles are shorter, you may opt to cast all of the stitches onto one longer straight needle. Once all of the stitches have been cast on, divide them evenly between four of the DPNs. To divide the stitches, hold the needle with the cast-on stitches in your left hand, as if to knit. Using a DPN, insert the tip of the needle into the first stitch as if to purl. Slip the stitch to the right-hand needle. Continue to slip stitches as if to purl until the stitches are divided evenly over four needles. The remaining DPN is for knitting.

Working in the Round with Double-Pointed Needles

resource
GUIDE

ARTYARNS
39 Westmoreland Avenue
White Plains, NY 10606
914.428.0333
www.artyarns.com

DEBBIE BLISS & NORO YARNS
Distributed by Knitting
Fever International
P.O. Box 336
315 Bayview Avenue
Amityville, NY 11701
516.546.3600
www.knittingfever.com

FILATURA DI CROSA
Distributed by Tahki·Stacy Charles, Inc.
70–30 80th Street, Building 36
Ridgewood, NY 11385
800.338.YARN
www.tahkistacycharles.com

LANAKNITS DESIGNS
HEMP FOR KNITTING
Suite 3B, 320 Vernon Street
Nelson BC Canada V1L 4E4
888.301.0011
www.lanaknits.com

LION BRAND YARN CO.
135 Kero Road
Carlstadt, NJ 07072
800.258.YARN
www.lionbrand.com

LORNA'S LACES YARNS
4229 North Honore Street
Chicago, IL 60613
773.995.3803
www.lornaslaces.net

PEACE FLEECE
475 Porterfield Road
Porter, ME 04068
800.482.2841
www.peacefleece.com

ROWAN YARNS
Westminster Fibers, Inc.
165 Ledge Street
Nashua, NH 03063
800.445.9276

SCOUT'S SWAG
www.scoutsswag.com

home decor
INSPIRATION

Since this book is as much about decorating your home as it is about knitting, I thought I'd share some of the resources I use to get inspiration for styling my space. These magazines and Web sites will start you daydreaming about how you can make your home the best reflection of you.

MAGAZINES
There is no shortage of home decor magazines on the market today! From DIY to "Darling, let's ring up the decorator," there are magazines to fit every budget, taste and lifestyle imaginable. I also find architecture magazines very inspiring. Impeccably styled, they give me great ideas on how to arrange furniture and accessories.

DOMINO MAGAZINE
Every month I eagerly await the arrival of this magazine. Every issue is overflowing with beautiful goodies for the home. From pricey one-of-a-kind *objets d'art* to cool furniture available at big-name bargain stores, *Domino* is full of loads of great must-haves and interesting decorating ideas. My favorite section is "Editors' Cravings," where a theme is chosen, such as "60s Jet Set" or "Jazz Age Finery," and *Domino* editors pick some of their favorite finds that reflect the stated theme.

DWELL MAGAZINE
While *Dwell* is more of an architecture and design mag, it does a beautiful job when it comes to styling living spaces. From grass-covered houses to famed architect Philip Johnson's Glass House, you are sure to be intrigued. If you want a glimpse into the genius behind some of the most original homes in America, you will definitely want to give *Dwell* a gander.

OBJEKT INTERNATIONAL
Objekt International is a beautiful quarterly magazine devoted to interiors, architecture, gardens, art, antiques and design. Each issue is an essential reference piece for people who are seeking creative ideas for living. Their features on some of the most innovative and creative minds in the world, such as designer Veronica Etro, are truly awe-inspiring!

BLOGS AND WEB SITES

There are the people who make things, and there are the people who style things that other people make. In other words, they tell you where to place them in a room and how to get them to play nicely with the rest of the decor. This list primarily features the latter. Why? Because you already know how to knit unique and beautiful accessories for your home. Here's a little help just in case you are not sure where to put them or how to make them work with everything else!

APARTMENT THERAPY
http://www.apartmenttherapy.com/
The Apartment Therapy blog features product reviews, furniture classifieds and helpful Q&A, such as: "How do you hang curtains on a corner window?" It also hosts an annual Smallest Coolest Apartment contest. If you live in a small space, you will love the great ideas you find here!

DECOR8
http://decor8.blogspot.com/
Decor8 bills itself as "a quick fix for design addicts who love decorating their homes but find it challenging to shop online." This fabulous blog provides readers with product and shop reviews and alerts readers to sales and bargain finds. It also lists a design blog and a design book of the week. And there's more! The site features interviews with some of the most innovative minds working in craft and design.

DESIGNER'S LIBRARY
http://designerslibrary.typepad.com/
I am in love with Meg Mateo Ilasco's blog, Designer's Library. She has fantastic taste and a great eye for design. She posts pics from inspiring vintage design books and magazines, as well as offers features on fabulous new designers. If you are looking for an original idea on how to style your living space, this is the place to go!

DESIGN*SPONGE
http://designsponge.blogspot.com/
Grace Bonney of Design*Sponge definitely has her finger on the pulse of what's happening in the worlds of art, craft and design. Her up-to-the-minute reports on all things stylish keep me informed on the latest trends, ideas and products making waves worldwide.

STYLE COURT
http://stylecourt.blogspot.com
The savvy woman behind Style Court definitely knows her stuff. This is the place to go if you want to educate yourself on classic interior design and decorative arts. Her posts are well-researched, informative and inspiring.

INDEX

check out these other fabulous
KNITTING AND CROCHET TITLES FROM NORTH LIGHT BOOKS.

YarnPlay
BY LISA SHOBHANA MASON
YarnPlay shows you how to fearlessly mix yarns, colors and textures to create bold and graphic handknits. You'll learn how to draw from your yarn stash to create stylish, colorful knits, including sweaters, tanks, hats, scarves, blankets, washcloths and more for women, men and children. Best of all, you'll learn knitting independence—author Lisa Shobhana Mason believes in learning the rules so you can break them. She teaches you how to take a pattern and make it your own.
ISBN-13: 978-1-58180-841-4
ISBN-10: 1-58180-841-0
PAPERBACK, 128 PAGES, Z0010

DomiKNITrix
BY JENNIFER STAFFORD
Once you know the joys of disciplined knitting, you'll never look back. Let experienced knitter Jennifer Stafford help you whip your stitches into shape. This book features a no-nonsense, comprehensive guide to essential knitting operations and finishing techniques. In the second half of the book, you'll put your knitting know-how to the test with patterns for over 20 handknit projects to wear and gift, including a halter "bra-let," a contoured zipper vest, a Jughead hat, icon sweaters and even a knitted mohawk. Plus much, much more.
ISBN-13: 978-1-58180-853-7
ISBN-10: 1-58180-853-4
FLEXIBIND CASE, 256 PAGES, Z0171

Fitted Knits
BY STEFANIE JAPEL
Fitted Knits features 25 projects to fit and flatter. You'll learn how to tailor T-shirts, sweaters, cardigans, coats and even a skirt and a dress to fit you perfectly. Take the guesswork out of knitting garments that fit. The book includes a detailed section that shows you how to know when and where increases and decreases should be placed to create the most attractive shaping.
ISBN-13: 978-1-58180-872-8
ISBN-10: 1-58180-872-0
PAPERBACK, 144 PAGES, Z0574

These and other fine North Light titles are available at your local craft retailer or bookstore, at www.fwbookstore.com or from other online suppliers.